A BOOK FULL OF ROGEI

A Book Full of Rogersons

BARNABY ROGERSON

BARING & ROGERSON
LONDON

First published in Great Britain by Baring & Rogerson,
part of Eland Publishing Ltd, 61 Exmouth Market,
London, EC1R 4QL in 2021

ISBN 978 1 900209 20 5

Text edited by Rosemary Gray
Text set in Great Britain by James Morris
Cover design by Rose Baring
Printed in England by CPI Antony Rowe

For Aunt Eve,
a childless woman, seldom seen
without a cigarette in one hand and a lipstick-kissed
glass of gin in the other,
who yet held her family together

Contents

Acknowledgements

Great-aunt Eve, cousin Phyllis and cousin Sidney Rogerson are acknowledged as the chief story-keepers in the text. I am also equally grateful to the shared enthusiasm of my second cousin Mathew Rogerson and my third cousin Jeremy Rogerson who freely shared with me the various letters, photographs and news clippings that they have carefully guarded and conserved for future generations. Olivia, my step grandmother, was faultless in keeping safe and then passing onto me anything to do with the Rogerson family unless it was money. All credit for unearthing the paper trail of four generations of Rogerson famers in 17th and 18th century belongs to two professional researchers, Dr Joanna Martin from Ipswich and Diana J Spelman from Norwich. They were diligent, professional and thoughtful, and I have kept hold of a file of their typed-up letters revealing their careful research into the rate-books, parish registers and wills of East Anglia, should anyone be interested in the details of this paper trail. Their modest fees were generously shared by my father in that pre-internet age and stretched over a leisurely period of correspondence between 1983 and 1998. My father did his very best to look interested in this historical research but like most Rogersons was interested in his cousins but not remotely intrigued by his ancestors. I have often wondered if this attitude is part and parcel of being English. My mother was passionate about her own family story but they had the advantage of being displaced from the romantic reaches of the British Isles, with Presbyterian Scots coming down from the hills to better themselves on her fathers side balanced by an Anglo-Irish tradition of foreign service on her mothers side.

I am also very grateful to Pippa Rogerson, Jenny Wills, Valda Embiricos, Alastair Nicolson, Andrea Rogerson, Guy Martin, Mary-Lou Hussey and Dinah Rogerson who responded to emails and corrected proofs or contributed stories and photographs. One of the happiest tasks in creating this family history has been interviewing my sister and two brothers. I thank them for their patience and hope they will accept these scribbles as some proof of my love and regard for them. The diversity of our politics, lifestyle and opinions always amused and occasionally baffled our parents. I also enjoyed trying to capture something of the spirit of my father and uncles, and to a lesser extent my grandfather and his two sisters and two brothers. I am aware that in doing this I have created a lopsided family story, that tunnels out a rather restricted vision from out of my own experiences and that of my immediate forbears. But this has the considerable advantage of allowing me to be as indiscreet as I wish. I have consciously been more respectful to other branches of the family, who I have listed in The Cousinage Appendix with unaccustomed brevity which is at least factual. I warmly commend the process of excavating old gossip to any cousin, if they wish to make their own expanded version centred on their own immediate family.

In the physical construction of this book, I am totally indebted to Rosemary Gray, who poured her considerable expertise as an editor and as a proof-reader, to make this book better. And to James Morris who made the words look beautiful on the page. Rose Baring prepared the cover with her customary skill and visual precision, which included repairing the scans of old photographs on her computer.

CHAPTER ONE

Hrothgar

There is a hunger, marrow deep, to know our heritage – to know who we are and where we came from.
Without this enriching knowledge, there is a hollow yearning. No matter what our attainments in life,
there is still a vacuum, an emptiness, and the most disquieting loneliness.
Alex Haley

The Rogersons are not a Celtic tribe, a Highland clan or a Border dynasty. We are an English family with five hundred years of history, most of it confined to the rural frontier of Suffolk and Norfolk. When Kirghiz nomads met in the grass steppelands of Central Asia, the first question they asked of each other was 'who are thy seven fathers?' Even an eight-year-old child will confidently be able to recite back seven generations. I think this is about right. I can recite the Rogerson patronymic back over fourteen generations, but I have noticed that the eyes of even the politest listener glaze over after seven generations. I am Barnaby Hugh (publisher and writer), third child of Keith Frank (Commander in the Royal Navy), who was the second son of Hugh Stanley (Commander in the Royal Navy and maltster) who was the second child of Frank (a London brewer who made a second fortune from insurance in the City of London), who was the seventh child of Josiah William (managing director of the Hoddesdon brewery), who was the second son of Charles Thomas (a farmer turned tea-merchant at Beccles), who was the son of Thomas Rogerson of Barsham Hall who was the last Rogerson to dirty his hands with farming. Then after this canonical seven, it goes on: Thomas was the son of William Rogerson (farmer at Narborough), who was the son of William Rogerson (farmer at Narford), who was the son of William Rogerson (farmer at Swaffham), who was the probable eighth child of Robert Rogerson (vicar of Denton), who was the son of Thomas Rogerson (vicar of Monks Soham deposed during the Civil war), who was the son of John Rogerson (vicar at Honingham). There is no flint tower beside a river in East Anglia that we can claim as our ancestral home, though the virtue of treating all children equally and pouring resources into their education is perhaps just as fine an inheritance. I own some letters and documents, a gold watch, a stick of furniture and a few oil paintings that have been passed down through a few generations of Rogersons. There is a seventeenth century Rogerson coat of arms, but it was registered by a cousin in Dublin, and under the strict rules of heraldry, we are squatters, if we make use of this.

The Rogerson family leans in the opposite direction to any aristocratic traditions of primogeniture, for it is the younger sons who have prospered and also quite often bagged the largest inheritance. So our family tree consistently leans offside. Frank Rogerson was the most financially successful of all the prosperous sons of Josiah, but he was child number seven. Michael Rogerson, who set up both Cottesmore School and the Cottesmore Golf club (creating a fine inheritance for his two sons), was Frank's fourth child, while the current headmaster (his grandson Thomas) is the youngest in his brood of siblings. Nico Rogerson (the charismatic founder of Dewe-Rogerson) was the youngest of the three sons of Hugh Rogerson. In my own generation, it is James Rogerson, the youngest of four children, who is proving himself much the most successful in business. During our youth, I very much doubt anyone would have put money on James, a charming polo-playing cavalry officer, becoming such a focused businessman. James has absolutely no interest in history (Rogerson, Roman or Islamic) but as I get older, I realise that he is a true representative of the breed. Brave and handsome, with a charming wide smile, he is also forever physically active, never seen with a book in his hands, but is a man who owns a dozen horses and who is now the dynamic, effervescent boss of hundreds of employees. There is no senior Rogerson line, no head of the family unless you earn that position through hospitality.

When you boast of your ancestors, it is like praising the potato, the best part of which remains underground

I have a Moroccan friend who has now lived for most of his life in London but travels all over the world to attend international conferences. He is a principled academic who runs a historical journal. He is just the sort of man to believe in the socio-economic definitions of class rather than have any truck with tribes and clans. I have known him long enough to ask some direct questions. This year I finally heard how hopeless and feckless his own father had been, and that it was his maternal uncles who had watched over his childhood and youth. They had supported their abandoned sister and enabled her to bring up her family as a single parent with dignity. My Moroccan friend is a Berber who was brought up in a poor household in a dry mountain district on the edge of the Sahara. He was emphatic that there was no one in Morocco who did not know which tribe they belonged to, even when living in the vast bustling coastal cities. And despite modern political parties and election campaigns these tribal loyalties retain their power. Every year, the sheikhs of the Moroccan tribes repeat their personal oath of loyalty to the king on the anniversary of his accession to the throne. I was delighted by this discovery.

In cultures where tribal identity is still a matter of economic and political importance it is usual for families to operate within the knowledge of six generations. Beyond six generations there is a nebulous cloud of ancestors, sometimes recorded in sketchy outline, but more often than not reduced to one heroic and distant ancestor. These totemic ancestors are respected, their tombs are often well maintained and made the centre of a yearly festival, but they are also highly versatile. They can be awarded extra sons and grandsons whenever

it is thought convenient to give a genealogical connection to some friendly neighbouring family or to help seal an alliance with some larger clan. It is a good system. You have the absolute support of your pre-ordained and unchangeable kinship group but you can also give free vein to sustaining flights of romantic fantasy and political co-option.

In Britain kinship is now a matter of taste rather than use. Most families operate within a memory range of just three generations. This provides a child with at least two parents, four grandparents and enough aunts, uncles and cousins to provide an ample variety of character, example, social range and story-telling. To stretch living (as opposed to written) memory back another generation is easy enough for the old but more difficult for the young. Memories become overloaded with sixteen equal great-great-grandparents to distinguish and family stories inevitably lose their central focus. If you march back further into the past the whole relevance of family characteristics and inherited genetic identity burns out into an alarmingly accelerating explosion of numbers. If you go back eight generations (to the time of coach horses and George III our farmer King) the rewards of examining any one individual are already very slight. For we have two hundred and fifty-six equally relevant ancestors from that generation, not just one heroic role model. In a way this is rather wonderful, for a proper understanding of the complexity of ancestry undermines any basis for racial pride, caste or social snobbery. The current state of medical research seems to be going in the opposite direction, as we realise that our susceptibility to diseases is ever more embedded within our inherited DNA. However, one would have to be absolutely certain of the biological connections to make a historical study of genetically inheritable strengths and susceptibilities worthwhile. And from a conversation that I once had with a nurse in a busy London hospital, one can see why this avenue of documentary research is unlikely to be pursued by the medical profession. Thirty years ago, this London hospital stopped taking blood samples from all males after in-house tests revealed that a third of babies had no genetic link with their proud fathers. Even the modern spin on ancestry research, the DNA test, has it flaws that make it a dangerous tool beyond five generations. Our DNA cannot lie but it can hide. For it is such a highly random matter, as to which strips of genetic material get copied into eggs and sperm, that it is totally possible that one particular great, great grandparent can virtually disappear from the genetic evidence.

So there is no scientific argument for family history but it yet has an important purpose. It balances the greater events of national and international history against a humdrum catalogue of everyday human affairs. Instead of battles and conquests, changes of regime and dynasties, a family story keeps a much saner focus. It is not a legend of the decline and fall of kingdoms, but a simple story of survival: chronicled by marriages, children, houses lived in, jobs, wills and gravestones. At its very simplest, it is a chronicle of fertile fucks. So the central figures of this narrative are not heroic explorers but fecund mothers and middle-aged hands-on, stay-at-home dads. All others eventually get airbrushed out of the record, such as the daughters who change their surname, as well as the more intrepid characters who travelled, died young or devoted their lives to faith, charity or scholarship – let alone the 'black sheep' that catch-all explanation for socially invisibility, usually for the crime of being gay, marrying out of class or becoming poor.

This book is an attempt to hold on to some stories. To retain some of the animating gossip which made the Rogerson family interesting to me as a child. To recount some tales and share some myths from the past. The year of 2020 has unexpectedly provided me with the freedom to set about this. It has been an unusual year. I have found it interesting to observe how quickly things can revert, even under the mildest of worldwide plagues. We have once again learned that our precious carapace of civilisation is separated from anarchy by just three meals. And we have been reminded of the madness of crowds, by the empty shelves caused by hoarding. But it is also reassuring to see how old loyalties have so quickly returned to prominence, in the rediscovery of neighbours, and, above all, it has proved that when the chips are down the family remains the elemental structure.

It is easy to translate Rogerson. We are the 'son of Roger.' As a child-genealogist I lived in the hope of finding some heroic first Roger who would be the ancestor of all the Rogersons in Britain. We could then become a tribe and have clan gatherings on a hill fort on midsummer's day. This hope evaporated when I learned more about the name Roger. It is of Norse origin (the Vikings and the Danes) and means 'famous spear'. It was a flattering epithet given to a warrior by his admiring comrades. Roger is the shortened form of *hrothgar*, a word of Germanic origin created by combining two words, *hroth* (fame) and *gar* (spear). To 'roger' is yet another word for 'fuck', and there is also a phallic connotation to Hrothgar. This would have delighted my grandfather who liked to explain that the way to understand a Rogerson was to be aware that they kept their moral compass in their trousers. The early Norman conquerors of England, who were Norse (and only partly civilised by living in France for a few generations), were particularly fond of Roger as a given name. The chronicles of the eleventh and twelfth century are full of hard-headed, ambitious Norman knights called Roger who seize baronies or southern kingdoms for themselves. By the time the first surnames begin to be written down in Britain we already find a good crop of FitzRogers, Rogesouns and Rogersons spread all around the country.

What is useful is the tenacity of our form of spelling Rogerson over the last five centuries. I have found out that Rogerson families come from five areas: from the east coast of Scotland, from Durham and Northumberland, from Dumfries in south-west Scotland, from Lancashire (where they have tended to be Catholics) and from East Anglia. This remains as true today as it was in the thirteenth century, as any glance at a British telephone directory will inform you, while in conversation with emigrants I have found these areas get referenced as the home-ground. They are all either on the east coast (the main area of Norse settlement) or came under the influence of the Norse principality of Man. Numerically, Lancashire and its cities have the thickest spread of individuals. Our lot came from East Anglia and are numerically the weakest on the ground.

I once read a claim that we could be descended from the FitzRoger family. They were one of the recognized merchant clans of *Franci homines* whose names pop up in the contents of the Hundred Rolls (that litany of rights, land tenure, and court cases). The FitzRogers were a contentious lot locked in rivalry with the neighbouring merchants of Dunwich, Walberswick and Yarmouth. Their own base was the marshland of Blythburgh. There was also a Ralph Rogerson executed in the ditch of Norwich Castle for opposing King Henry VIII's suppression of the holy pilgrimage to the Abbey of Our Lady of Walsingham in Norfolk. I would love to claim Ralph as a cousin (both a radical, a reactionary, a rebel and a martyr) who died in defence of a shrine raised to honour an apparition of the Mother of God, but this ambition has yet to be achieved.

Another family distinction – which first revealed itself over the last two world wars among a merry ricochet of misdirected restaurant accounts and tailors bills that went bouncing between the various Rogersons - was a taste for the same given names: John, Thomas and William. The same names occur again and again throughout the centuries, though it is no doubt explainable by the need to scan elegantly with a three-syllable surname rather than any hidden memory of a common ancestor. But it was because of this that completely separate Rogerson families made connection with each owing to a prolonged muddle over mess bills. It was thus that my great uncle John Rogerson (serving as an ADC to an American general in London) and Colonel William Rogerson in Italy (his cousin) came across Colonel William Rogerson and his son Captain John Rogerson from Dumfrieshire, and with Colonel John Rogerson from Ashton-under-Lyne, Lancashire and Captain William Rogerson from Holywood Hall, Durham. There were even some exchange visits, and so we learned about a pack of foxhounds at Mount Oswald in County Durham, known as Rogerson's Hounds, as well as about a Dr John Rogerson from Dumfrieshire who served Catherine the Great of Russia and raised his family to fame, title and fortune. These are not our stories.

A Photographic Gallery of Rogersons, A–V

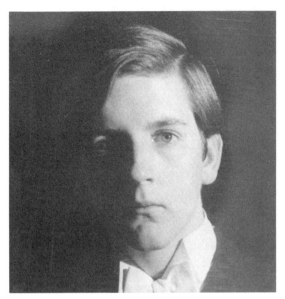

Andrea Rogerson (born 1950),
second son of Major Bill Rogerson

Barry Rogerson on Silver Skill

Aunt Eve (born 1897) amongst other bridesmaids at her brothers' wedding, at Brompton Oratory in 1925. From left to right: Prue
Russell, Judy Leveson-Gower, Freda Cotton, Jack Hunter, Mary Gerard, Evelyn Rogerson (Mrs Sandy Smith) and Thea Wallis.

Barry Hugh Rogerson, son of Cdr Hugh Rogerson in the uniform of a Lieutenant in the Irish Guards, Colchester barracks, 1947

David Rogerson, down Margaret Shaft, Stilfontein, Western Transvaal, South Africa, October 1984

Carlotta Rogerson winning the Swiss Young Riders Championship (Basel, 2017) on Dylan

Dido Rogerson as a bridesmaid, holding the hand of her cousin Jennifer Milligan, Mrs Richard Wills

Hugh Rogerson (born 1900), Cdr, Royal Navy, son of Frank Rogerson

Hugh taking a fence on Gone Gay, *Enfield Hunt steeplechase*

Gertrude Rochford on her wedding to Hugh Rogerson

Frank Rogerson (1872–1946)

Florence Allenby, Mrs Frank Rogerson, born 1877.

Jeremy Rogerson, Cdr Royal Navy, son of
Col Sidney Rogerson

James Rogerson, Queens Own Hussars

Wedding of Tessa Crimmin and Jeremy Rogerson

Josiah Rogerson (1832–1903) with Lucy-Maria and their nine children: back row from left, Arthur, Mini, Louisa, Jack; middle row from left Charlie, Josiah, Lucy-Maria, Sidney; bottom row from left Frank, Herbert, Harry.

Wedding of Kathleen Harvie and Keith Rogerson

Sir John Rogerson (1648-1724) variously Lord Mayor, M.P. and High Sheriff of Dublin and father of John Rogerson (1646-1741) Lord Chief Justice of Ireland

John Rogerson escorting Princess Elizabeth around the paddock at Hurst Park, February 1957

Keith Frank Rogerson (1928-2004), Commander, Royal Navy with his basset hounds

Mathew Rogerson, pageboy at wedding of his cousin Valda Rogerson and Tim Nicolson

Michael Rogerson (born 1910), third headmaster of Cottesmore School after Geoffrey Davison-Brown and Harry Strong-Forster

Wedding of Mathew Rogerson to Susan Cheeseman, 31 July 1950

Nico Rogerson standing above Roddy Dewe,
co-founders of Dewe-Rogerson

Sam Rogerson in front of Cottesmore; pageboy to his uncle
Mathew, wearing the same kilt that Mathew had worn for
the marriage of Valda Rogerson

Nico Rogerson exercising his father's polo ponies: front four – starting the left; Chime, Apero (ridden), Tobasco, Rich Tea;
back three – starting from left; Choir, Molymolines, Pimms.

Pippa Rogerson: 43rd Master of Gonville & Caius College (and the first woman), mother of five pony-loving Fitzsimon daughters who also teaches law at Cambridge University, concentrating on international commercial disputes.

The Reverend Sidney Rogerson, 1867–1957

Colonel Sidney Rogerson (1894–1968) about to be introduced at Court with his father in law, Sir Henry Gibson

Valda Rogerson winning the Newmarket Town Plate on Vulpes, October 1958

CHAPTER TWO

Telling Stories

My sense of family history is somewhat sketchy, because mother kept a great deal to herself.
Julie Andrews

I first became interested in family stories when I was very young, for they were in the air I breathed. Both my parents had lost their mothers when they were aged ten, and their loss was quickly followed in both cases by the disappearance of their fathers. My mother's father (who had served in the cavalry throughout the First World War) and my father's father (who had served in the Royal Navy) were both called up as reservists and served throughout the duration of the Second World War as well. Both my parents were effectively orphaned, but help was at hand. Their uncles and aunts stepped up and tried to fill the gaps. Both my parents formed lifelong bonds of affection and gratitude.

This precocious interest in family stories was further encouraged by my schooling. I was educated between the ages of seven and thirteen at Cottesmore, a very English boarding school that was owned and run by my great uncle, Michael Rogerson. At times it seemed quarter-filled with Rogerson cousins and connections. Michael Rogerson was an eccentric and hospitable man. He was hyperactive, a perpetual schoolboy, passionate about all sports, very keen on activities and France. On Sundays we were encouraged to speak French at meals and we certainly sang La Marseillaise with greater gusto than God Save the Queen. If the weather was warm on a Sunday morning, he would wake all the boys up, and we would run in our dressing gowns to have a swim in the lake. On more than one occasion he arranged for a Spitfire to bomb the cricket pitches with sweets. He also had a bit of a cult following, for during the confusing years at the beginning of the Second World War he had taken the entire school off into the Welsh Hills, and effectively become the avuncular father-figure to several dozen children who had been separated from their parents. He also had been very understanding about unpaid bills, especially sons whose fathers were away at war. He was very fortunate in that his wife (Aunt Marion) knew how to run a school, as her own Brownrigg father had been the owner-manager of Fernden, a similar private school. Many of the best things about Cottesmore came through Aunt Marion. My elder brother reminded me two examples from our childhood: how she helped the boys make elderberry wine, which was served at the Christmas dinner and how she provided dough so that we could make bread in the underground stove we had invented in a labyrinth of 'escape' tunnels dug into the sandstone below the cricket pitch. She ran the school kitchens using students from a Danish village who for decades had come to improve their English under her safe watch. Nantie, a benign but ancient matron, had unique authority. She had started off in 1915 as the childhood nurse of Aunt Marion and looked after three generations of her family (as well as taking time out to have her own life, running a village store between 1935-46) before taking on the care of eighty boys in retirement. Her upstairs sitting room was filled with jigsaws and old packs of cards and kept at a baking temperature by a blazing coal fire. She ended up in her own house on the Cottesmore estate for her husband, David Challis, died in 1952. David did a bit of chauffeuring but his health had never really recovered from being gassed during the war

Cottesmore was an impressive building (a Pont Street Dutch mansion plonked on a Sussex hillside) and it allowed Michael Rogerson to host a stream of relatives, inviting them for drinks in his study or to join in the vast tea laid out in the main hall every afternoon or to spend the night in one of the many spare bedrooms. So even if you did not go to school at Cottesmore, it was one of the key social centres of the Rogerson family. Even before he turned the home farm into a golf course, he had made a smaller golf course for the use of the school and there were a number of grass tennis courts and a lake enclosed by woodland. Cottesmore was also easy to get to, halfway between London and Brighton and just a few miles from Gatwick Airport.

Even as a boy I realised that there were multiple answers to any single question. I was aware that our own grandfather loved to mock his younger brother, so as a seven-year-old boy looking up at the cane-wielding master of my universe, the headmaster of Cottesmore, M. D. Rogerson, M.A., I could also hear in the back of my head, the peppery voice of my naval grandfather shouting, 'Here comes that bloody fool Michael and his smelly feet.' My grandfather also liked to dismiss anyone living south of the Thames as 'suburban Surrey sods' and self-identified himself as the only true Rogerson, living in the land of his ancestors, working the soil as a farmer and involved in the traditional family business of brewing beer and malting barley. His home was always filled with dogs, which in our era of knowing him meant that the sofa was covered in a sea of dachshunds, and there was a refreshing amorality about him with an instinctive understanding that sexuality was your own affair. Although untouched by homophobia, our grandfather could indulge in a verbal vendetta against those flannelled fools who preferred to play ball games instead of risking their necks out hunting. So his children and grandchildren were much more familiar with the punch-lines from Surtees's Jorrocks (a scruffy London tea merchant who was passionate about hunting) than with the verses of the Bible. One of my grandfather's more aggressive retorts, when asked if he would like to join in a game of tennis or a round of golf, was 'I haven't finished fucking my wife yet'. Another favourite remark was 'the only pair of balls I will ever hit will be when I stand on a rake'. This line of thinking was continued by my own father, another outspoken naval officer, and given a further twist by the noisy bargaining sessions that were sometimes held in the bar (wallpapered with hundreds of front covers of *Country Life* magazine) beside the drawing room at Cottesmore. For my father claimed that his uncle Michael had been given a double-helping of Frank Rogerson's fortune in order to support

the unprofitable business of running a school. In exchange he was to provide free education to all male Rogersons. The former allegation was agreed, but the latter clause was hotly denied. Nevertheless I think some sort of discount was agreed upon in the end. All of this helped to make me realise that family history could be interesting. This feeling was further encouraged by the occasional night-time visits of my great-aunt Eve. She was Michael Rogerson's older sister who made up her own rules for how to conduct life. It was her practice to stuff her handbag with contraband sweets and as she made the round of the dormitories, (smelling of scent and gin) demanding the right to kiss all her young relatives on their brow while furtively pushing an illegal contraband chocolate bar under their pillow. There was something about the shape of the back of my head that won her approval. It marked me out as a Rogerson. And one of the proudest moments of my childhood was when Aunt Eve was asked a question in a packed drawing room. She gave me a wink from her place on the sofa, and from her position of authority, replied 'Ask Barnaby, he is the family historian.'

As a nine-year-old family historian in the year of 1969, I was aware that there were three authorities within the family: Colonel Sidney in Suffolk, Cousin Phyllis in Cambridge and Great-Aunt Eve. The Rogerson family were not renowned for their love of literature, indeed I can remember my uncle damning a new neighbour by loudly explaining that he was 'the sort of man who reads books'. Sidney Rogerson not only read books but

Aunt Eve with her brother Michael and husband Sandy Smith.

Colonel Sidney Rogerson

wrote them. Years before he had sent out a round-robin letter to all his cousins, seeing if they wanted to join together and share in the cost of a researcher, to link up the missing generations with our ancestors buried at Denton church in Norfolk. I don't think anyone replied, but whenever I asked for detailed information this unanswered letter would be pulled out of a draw. When I asked my grandfather about a family tree he looked appalled, and told me that was the sort of question you might expect from an American or an Australian but he had no need of such a thing, for he knew exactly who he was, where he belonged and who his family was. No one seemed to know what had become of Sidney Rogerson's papers. He had collected pictures as a young man, but in his old age had been forced to sell them. Cousin Phyllis was old but still very alive. She was not friends with her cousin Eve and they had different family histories to tell. Over years of letter-writing, Cousin Phyllis forwarded me copies of tombstone inscriptions from old churchyards in Norfolk and Suffolk, and charts full of clergymen who had all studied at Cambridge and married into county families. It was clear that in her mind,

a true Rogerson lived in East Anglia and dedicated himself to the Church of England. Her father and her husband had both been clergymen.

Aunt Eve had a more lively view of family life of which she was the active lynch-pin. She had a twinkle to her eye and a wonderful tone to her voice, matured by cigarettes and gin and Dubonnet. She lived in London and had been brought up in a succession of large gin-swilling mansions in Surrey or Sussex that had been owned by her father, Frank Rogerson. Aunt Eve had a great devotion to her brothers and sister, who she would visit on biannual tours, but she also had an encyclopaedic memory for her extended family. The full extent of the latter was put to the test every winter in the dining room of her flat in London. Amidst the debris of her heavy smoking, her lipstick-kissed glasses of gin and Dubonnet and the racing pages of the papers she would assemble and wrap a mass of glittering presents for most of her known relations. She was a very good and generous present buyer, which in my case always included the instant fun of a Tintin book combined with the lasting value of a volume from the Oxford University Press *History of England*. These were not trusted to the Post Office but assembled into family piles and despatched into the hands of nephews and nieces and cousins as they came to call for a Christmas drink. For Aunt Eve the extended Rogerson family was a passion that replaced the children she had never had. She was an exact source of information about the present state of her family to the third cousin-age as well as of her mother's Allenby family. She alone held on to the memory of the last proper farming Rogerson, growing barley and ploughing the fields around Barsham Hall in Suffolk with his own team of horses. She also told me the more romantic tale of the penniless Cavalier who first brought fame and fortune to the Rogerson family by loyally serving his Stuart prince. It was Francis Rogerson's task to chat up the jolliest wenches working in the inns of Holland and France and then to find out in bed which ones were most likely to amuse his master, who was the exiled (and penniless) Prince Charles. Rogerson exhausted himself in his devotion to this royal duty and would be buried in a pauper's grave in Holland. But his old comrades in exile looked after his orphaned son, who would be sent to Cambridge alongside his Norfolk cousins. They were not forgotten when the

Cavaliers returned in triumph at The Restoration. It was not a morally suitable tale for young children, but she and my father could quote 'improper stories' from Saki as if they were the gospel truth. Aunt Eve shared in the high spirits of this dashing but possibly mythical Rogerson ancestor. She had been the mistress of Sir Edward Mountain, a successful financier (who was also a close business associate of her father). In her heyday Eve had owned and run a fashionable boutique near Bond Street named Anne Blake in South Moulton street where William Blake had once lived. Her nephew Barry Rogerson would follow her example, becoming first the lover, then the husband of the wife of his father's business partner - Richard Page-Croft.

Aunt Eve's circuit of travels, staying not for the weekend but for weeks in the houses of her brothers and sister, was dictated by the racing season. Her brother Hugh Rogerson, her nephew Barry Rogerson, her niece Valda and her sister-in-law Eileen were all talented amateur jockeys. Eileen Rogerson won the Newmarket Town Plate, while on one spectacular day in 1953 Barry Rogerson rode four successive winners at the Puckeridge and Thurlow Point to Point steeplechases at Wickham Hall. Aunt Eve's brother John and his wife Eileen had their own stable of racing horses (with different racing colours for Mr John Rogerson and Mrs John Rogerson) and at various periods in their life, her brother Hugh and her sister Betty also tried to keep up with this glamour, and owned race horses with their own racing colours. Aunt Eve's niece Valda would continue this tradition and owned horses that won the St Leger and the Grand National. As a boy I observed that Racing (there was never any need to define it any further than that) was a passion that united the entire Rogerson family. It was combined with betting and booze to make an all-powerful trinity of amusements. Once the television had been invented, it was a recognisable feature of any Rogerson household to have several screens permanently switched on over the afternoon, so that different race meetings could be observed all over the country.

When we stayed with our Rogerson relatives we never met an Aunt or a Great Aunt before 11.30 in the morning. They would take their breakfast in bed, slowly puttig their face on while they studied 'the form.'. Only when they had placed their bets with their trusted bookies by telephone, to cover a spread of the Day's Races, would they descend and join their guests. Our childhood was filled with long journeys to various race courses, but my father made it fun by telling us jokes as he drove, and once there he allowed us to perch on the roof rack for a better view, even if we were made to wear tweed breeches. Basket work picnic hampers overflowing with homemade scotch eggs, flasks of soup and bottles cascaded out from the back of cars. Bowler hats had already gone out of fashion but would still be worn by our great-uncle John Rogerson or our uncle Barry Rogerson, marking them out as either stewards or fence-inspecting officials of The Jockey Club.

Aunt Eve married Uncle Sandy, a devoted old admirer, and together they lived in a flat in Bentinck street, near the Wallace Collection on Manchester Square. Sandy Smith spoke with a broad Scottish accent and did not mind Aunt Eve's colourful past or their own lack of children. Aunt Eve was beloved by all her younger relations. Her niece Valda sent me this e-mail in response to a photograph,

"I loved Auntie Eve. She was so kind to me. I stayed a lot with her in her flat off Welbeck Street. She was a very good dressmaker and made our bridesmaids dresses for Aunt Betty and Uncle Pat's wedding. When Tim was ill in the hospital for tropical diseases, I stayed with her for her over a week to be nearby to visit. So I took a week's course at the Cordon Bleu school in Marylebone Lane. It didn't much improve my cooking skills! Oh, how this brought back so many memories. Sorry to bore you, but I was so fond of her."

Not all women, especially from her own generation held her in high esteem. Her sister-in-law, Olivia Rogerson awarded her the derogatory nickname 'brillo pad', in mocking reference to Eve's perm of jet-black dyed hair. It was Olivia who also first circulated the rumour that Eve had herself "tied up" as a young woman in order to have as many lovers as she desired. Olivia was our step-grandmother and was possessed of a splendidly wicked tongue and an engaging vivacity for life. By the time we knew her she no longer admired her husband. Later on, I found out that she had never forgiven him for giving her a dose of the clap which he had picked up from a London prostitute after a boozy lunch at the South London Hop Exchange.

All her love was poured on to her only child, our Uncle Nico, and she became an amusingly hostile witness to the Rogerson family. They could be pompous, self-regarding and complacent as a clan and needed pricking with her wit. Her family also came from East Anglia; she had a brother (Bill Worthington) in the Navy and an intellectual sister, a pioneer psychiatrist called something like Mary Barton. Olivia provided 'context' and as she was not interested in anything to do with the Rogerson family she generously passed all items on to me. But we realised it was always much more fun being visited by our grandfather Hugh without her. We knew him as 'Pop'; he was always immaculately dressed and drove fast cars, tipped us with silver crowns, flirted with barmaids and bought us illegal drinks. Our home was always a bit shabby, so he preferred to stay in the nearest pub which also allowed him to be the host. When we visited him in his home in Suffolk, he was not nearly such fun. The static of animosity between husband and wife made it feel like walking into a Thurber cartoon. When Olivia thought it was time for Commander Hugh Rogerson to be moved into a nursing home (the better to care for his asthma), my grandfather went upto his dressing room. Having packed his bag, he lay down on his single bed in his best pinstripe grey suit and pulled a plastic bag over his head.

I was always proud of how well my father continued to treat his stepmother subsequently whatever she got up to in terms of anti-Rogerson propaganda. On this occasion he at once drove over to Suffolk to help her sort things out and found a succession of wills (each one giving him and his elder brother less and less money), but kept this information to himself. Many decades later I attended Olivia's funeral in Suffolk and accepted a lift back to London with Nico Rogerson's business partner. He also gave a free ride to Olivia's oldest surviving female friend in his chauffeur-driven car. Perhaps a kinder man than Roddy Dewe would not have been so persistent, but it was his genius to be always extracting information. He coaxed Olivia's ancient, doddery old friend into talking about their youth together, for they had shared a cottage and had been rumoured to have been girlfriends.

'No, Olivia never loved Hugh, but she wanted a house and pretty dresses, so she had to marry him.'

'No, she would not sleep with him before their marriage, he had a reputation you know.'

'No, she never really cared for those stepsons, such sad little lost boys. What were their names…. something ugly I remember, like Barry and Keith?'

I tried to look amused but felt sad on behalf of my father and uncle. Sometimes you get to learn too much family history.

CHAPTER THREE

Begin with the Living

Preserve your memories, keep them well, what you forgot you can never tell.
Louisa May Alcott

The usual way of telling a family story is to begin in the far distant past, and then proceed down the generations towards your own time. The more I thought about this, the more I realised that it is in complete reversal to how we actually think about such things. The family you know about are all packed into the immediate three generations that surround you. And then ever diminishing ripples of interest stretch out your distant ancestors and relations.

So I shall begin with the living, then slowly work back to the past. This was also the emphatic advice of a local historian I met many years ago, who was insistent that you should only advance from the secure bedrock of what you know. In his particular case he had immersed himself in the history of his Scottish Highland clan and only towards the end of his life did he discover that he had been adopted from out of an Irish orphanage. His advice was to begin with yourself. Accept nothing on trust, for if you cannot locate your own birth certificate and the marriage register entry for your own parents, why do you think excavating the deeper past is going to be any easier.

My sister **Dido (Diana Mary Rogerson)** was born on 16 December 1955. She is the eldest of our parents' family of four and was born in a military hospital in Singapore. She then spent a couple of months in Hong Kong before journeying by ship with her mother back to England. Theirs was one of the last boats allowed through the Canal before the Suez Crisis – which put a rocket in the bows of the ship that her father was then serving in.

Dido inherited the full measure of Rogerson energy. Let me give you an example. We had all been travelling together in a minibus through southern Venezuela. The distances were vast, and so it had taken two solid days and a night of driving to reach my brother's home in El Callao. We were in a state of exhausted, but there was a party being given by a near neighbour (they actually lived two hours' drive away) which we knew we should really all attend. When we arrived at this isolated farmhouse, which stood in the shade of a vast protective tree, we all felt truly shattered. Dido just took a deep breath, put on a gash of red lipstick and stepped out of the car determined to make the evening work. Within minutes she was greeting everyone, hugging her hostess and making enthusiastic connections. Watching Dido from a hammock proved to be more energising than cocaine, and so by the end of the evening we were all dancing.

Perhaps there is now a school that could constructively tap this sort of energy, but it did not exist in Dido's childhood. She was expelled from a succession of schools and at sixteen escaped into real life. Studying art at Sheffield University was combined with giving birth to a daughter in Portsmouth, then there followed a period in London as a flamboyant dress-designing, clubbing, film-making free spirit. I remember visiting her

Dido, Diana Mary Rogerson

gothick stall selling bone jewellery in Kensington Market before having a picnic in Hyde Park. She was an inspiring role model - don't just dream it, do it. Then I saw her in North London after the arrival of her second daughter (Lilith), nursing her child before a blazing coal fire, with the metal frame of an old piano echoing to every sound. She took one look at my girlfriend and welcomed her as a fellow Sagittarius. Her boyfriend, Steven Stapleton, was one of the pioneers of British industrial music, produced under the *Nurse With Wound* label, as well as an experimental artist working out of a studio in Soho. Then came their decision to migrate from their North London flat to the West coast of Ireland. There were seasons on the road for Dido in her own gypsy wagon. More music, some drama interspaced with three more children (Louis, Luke and Django) while she and Steven restored the old cottage of Cooloorta into a sort of live-in sculpture which had the bathroom doubled-up as a cactus sanctuary and was surrounded by ponies, chickens, goats, donkeys, an eco-pond recycling grey water, a vegetable garden and blond free-range children. An old coach which let in lots of light was converted into a studio, and an old lorry was turned into a very romantic bedroom (draped with printed Indian cottons and Moroccan rugs) all tucked away into the surrounding woodland - overgrown nut coppice. Travelling families, a Spanish ballet dancer and her children, and a nomadic assortment of artists, writers and political radicals lived in nearby clearings. In the distance the limestone scarps of the Burren hills beckoned to the north, while to the south it was but a short stroll to swim in any of half a dozen lochs framed by old stone walls or overlooked by the broken stump of a medieval tower. When her children were older, Dido trained as a homeopathic healer, whilst at the same time trading in open-air markets, recording as a singer (CD's like *The Lights Are On But No-One's Home*) and working as an actress. She once tried her hand as a waitress, but her daughters begged her to give it up, as they began to hear excited tales from local friends about the worst waitress in the world and guessed who this might be. Over the last ten years I have been fortunate enough to walk the city of Galway, the Dingle Peninsula, the coast of Connemara and the Arran Isles with Dido as well as attend the marriage of her eldest child Ruby, who is a photographer who teaches art at university level. Ruby's wedding called out three days of hot sun. It was also a revelation of how the world could be - everything provided, created or

Dido with her children and a grandson at a blessing ceremony held in the ruins of Corcomroe Abbey below the Burren hills, Co Clare, Ireland. From left: Katherine Louise Ashling Wallis (Roo), Louis, Lili, Django, Luke, Freddie, herself.

given as a gift by her friends with love attached. Her two daughters are in no doubt about what a brilliant a grandmother (complete with adventures) Dido has become, though when they all get together, her five children often speculate about why Dido was always more of an older sister than a mother to them.

This is not such a mystery to her three brothers, who could recognise that although their own mother was devotedly attentive to her three boys, she was locked into something much more complicated and competitive with her only daughter. They had periods of total, near hysterical commitment to each other. Such as the time when my mother and Dido turned the kitchen into a chemistry lab for the manufacture of ethical, organic make-up (thirty years before this sort of thing became commercial). Or that summer in Virginia Beach when our beach hut of a home was given over to plastic basins filled with tie-died bundles of cotton. The resulted T-shirts which were then sold at an open-air stall beside the beach dunes, alongside waistcoats made from ring-pull cans, and belts from recycled machine-gun-shell cases. Dido's younger brothers were given the task of collecting used bullets from the swamp training ground used by the US Marine Corps. We were proud of our contribution, but they were incredibly heavy to wear as a belt, and so were more of a stall prop than a selling item. But aside from these times when they worked as a team, Dido and our mother fought. They were empowered by very different conceptions of the importance (or futility) of class, race and feminism.

But we were a family that could always be united by a shared delight in drink, picnics and dance, offset by the freedom of sitting for hours in silent contemplation of nature or a bonfire. One of the many useful things our parents taught us all was the pleasure of night-time walks. Not only so that we did not become afraid of the dark, but so that we could delight in the sounds and differences, of a world cleansed of accustomed noise.

David Keith Rogerson was born in Gosport, Hampshire (opposite the naval base of Portsmouth) on 12 February 1957. He was christened on the quarter deck of *HMS Puma* four months later, for it was feared that he might fade away. David was born a coeliac and only survived through my mother's passionate nursing. He was always as thin as a rake as a child, despite a bottle of beer at lunch to help build him up. But even as a boy he had a wonderfully inventive mind allied to clever hands. From my earliest years I can remember homemade chariots (which I was allowed to pull as a stand-in pony) and complex designs for The Barrell (which could travel through space and underwater) before he went on to make his own water-wheel generator (from a broken washing machine) and used an old motor-mower to power a go-cart (which was sadly taken off the road by the local policeman).

My brother's memories of his childhood begin with the two years in Rosyth (the naval base opposite Edinburgh in Scotland) and hearing the bagpipes on a green hill behind our depressing home. Then two years on the island of Malta when he was aged between six and eight. He could not understand a word of what was spoken in the school but he has happy memoires of Benjamin, an enormous rabbit that lived in the back of our sofa, and his father watering orange trees in big terracotta pots in the back garden. He vividly remembers the Seventh Destroyer Squadron sweeping into the Grand Harbour of Malta at full speed, the dropping their anchors to swing back like a line of choreographed dancers.

Back in England he was briefly schooled at Denmead (a village in Hampshire) where once again he was an alien sitting at the back of the class. Then he was sent off to boarding school, to Cottesmore (the prep school run by our great-uncle Michael Rogerson) from 1965-70, then Charterhouse 1970-76 where he ended up as the headboy of his house, Verites. David then travelled across Australia over 1976 before spending three years studying geography at Durham University (1977-80). Like many young men, he found the period after university a bit of a shock, for the well-oiled pressures of the English educational system had suddenly finished with him.

David opted to work, as a farm labourer in Hampshire in order to fund his travels around South Africa, after which he applied to join the Royal Naval Hydrographic service, but in this he was frustrated by breaking his back (falling off a barn roof) and discovery of a mild degree of colour blindness. In 1981 he applied to join the South African Ordnance Survey and took up this post in September. After a years's traineeship, he left to work in the gold and diamond mines - for Stillfontein Gold and De Beers, from 1982-87. The

Apartheid system was still in operation, and the mines were a toxic taste of real life but this is where David made all his important lifelong friendships. In 1985 his parents came over to explore South Africa and he noticed how things had changed.

David Rogerson with his survey tripod, South America

His father was no longer judgemental but accepted him as a man, and for the first time they became friends, 'really good company on the road, incredible experience, uncritical.'

David took the chance opportunity to work in Venezuela in the summer of 1988 but liked what he saw and decided to stay on. For the first three years he worked for Monarch Resources, then set up two companies with Guy Martin based on El Callao. SURCO was their mineral-survey company which was allied to Servicios Mineros, which provided logistical support. They ran this together until 2001, when Guy took his young family back to England. David stayed on, for he had fallen in love with a Venezuelan geologist, Ysbelia Briceno. They built their own house, pool and garden, and brought up Wilfredo together. Then having bought a farm David spent three years fencing his own cattle ranch before political anarchy in 2016 made this venture impossible. He returned to freelance survey work (working in gold mines in Colombia and Mexico) and also designed and built a series of gold processing works in Venezuela. Confined to his walled garden by covid 19, he put this period to good use by digging a 20 metre well to tap his own water source. The excavated material baked into bricks with which he made an outdoor oven.

David with his SURCO team of Venezuelan surveyors, which includes his business partner, Guy Martin

Guy Martin gave a very good speech at David's wedding which I have filleted down

Nothing prepares you for a deep level gold mine. No amount of training on the surface makes you ready for the thunderous decent into a mine that is nearly 3000 metres deep. The calamity of noise from Rock Hoists, from the triple deck cages carrying 180 men at a time, and from the drilling - is overwhelming. The confined spaces of the Stopes and the ore-passes where surveyors have to work and the stifling, breath-sapping heat only serve to exacerbate this assault on the senses. It is this environment – David likes to describe it as 'where God hands over to the Devil' – that helped develop the characteristics of perseverance and determination that are so manifest in David's personality to say nothing of his stubbornness and single-mindedness. After years of hard study in South Africa David earned his Mine Survey Ticket – no mean feat in itself – followed by a spell in the Diamond mines of the North-West Cape. It was in 1988 that David found himself as a Consultant Mine Surveyor at Minerven Gold Mine in El Callao, Venezuela.

In 1989 I joined David in Venezuela and realised that it was not just the lure of US Dollars that was attracting David. Enter stage-left: Ysbelia Briceno ! To say that I was surprised that David had landed such a beautiful catch would be unfair … unfair but nevertheless true. So who was this amazing Venezuelan lady that had captured David's heart?

Ysbelia's grandfather had come to El Callao from St. Lucia - like many of his contemporaries from the Lesser Antilles – to work for the British gold mining companies that operated around El Callao during the early part of the last century. Her father Tomás and his brothers all started out on the mines but saved up and all bought Taxis as a means to escape the inhospitable conditions underground. Ysbelia is part of a rich Caribbean culture in El Callao that at Carnival time draws in partygoers from all over the country. But Ysbelia is not just a pretty face. David met Ysbelia at Minerven Mine where she was working as a Senior Engineering Geologist having previously qualified at the University of Caracas.

In those early days David and I shared a Breezeblock house with a Corrugated tin roof. It was a Spartan affair and to liven up the décor we filled the kitchen shelves with empty Whisky and Wine bottles. However these bottles looked like they were full and had attracted the attention of some local youths. One night David awoke to the sounds from the kitchen. He armed himself with a pick-axe handle and confronted three knife-wielding men who had peeled back the roof and climbed in searching for liquor. He took all three on and succeeded in chasing them back out through the same hole in the roof that they had used to enter.

I had slept soundly through the whole event - until I felt a firm prod in the back. I opened my eyes and rolled over to be confronted by David in just his boxer shorts and with a Pick-Axe handle in his hands. When I asked what the hell was going on he just said, "We've had visitors"!!

Many of you here who have known David longer than I have will know of his affection for gardening and animals but you might not know of his mechanical expertise with cars?

By 1991 I had joined David as a partner in SURCO our very own Surveying Services Company. The second car we bought was a pea-green long wheelbase Toyota Land Cruiser – known as La Iguana – and this car was taking some time to learn to obey David. On one particular morning we had loaded it with crew and equipment and progressed about 300 yards to the centre of the market square in El Callao when it packed in. David was livid and leapt out of the drivers seat and circled the car lambasting it with his finest Anglo-Saxon expletives and kicking it fervently - all this much to the embarrassment of the workers on-board and to the amusement of

David Rogerson marries Ysbelia Briceno, an event staged in two continents

the merchants and shoppers at the market stalls. But I promise you – when he got back in – the car started!!

David is usually extremely calm under pressure but he is not averse to a bit of theatre if it will have the desired effect … and the famous 'Rogerson Hat Fling' is one of the weapons in his armoury. Most of the hats David has owned have been flung down, stamped on and sworn at to accentuate a point he might be trying to make to a hapless bull-dozer driver or a civil engineer who hasn't quite come round to David's point of view.

On one particular occasion I had the pleasure of watching a Hat Fling through a Theodolite from the relatively safe distance of about quarter of a mile away. My survey assistants and I took turns watching David through the telescope – it was like a silent movie and when the hat eventually came off and was lashed to the floor a great cheer went up from the Crew. As a business partner, in David I could not have wished for a more honourable, trustworthy and principled man. We have worked together

in some of the most hostile surveying environments on the planet – and we are still friends!

I would just like to say a few words in Spanish for Ysbelia:

'Estoy muy agradezido Ysbelia que has tenido la fe y la paciencia para esperar tanto tiempo por este matrimonio. Agradezido porque David es un gran amigo mio – el es honourable, decente, leal, fiel y generoso y el merece tu amor. El ha tenido la buena fortuna de conseguir, en usted, una mujer bella con las mismas virtudes. Espero que pasan el resto de sus vidas con amor, amistad y prosperidad'

'I am very grateful Ysbelia that you had the faith and patience to wait so long for this marriage. Grateful because David is a good friend of mine - he is honourable, decent, loyal, faithful and generous and deserves your love. He has had the good fortune to find you, a beautiful woman with the same virtues. I hope you spend the rest of your lives with love, friendship and prosperity.'

I was conceived during Cowes week, when my father was serving in the guard ship provided by the Royal Navy. He and my mother were going to the Corinthian Ball, but my mother looked so stunning in her black dress that she was delayed in the bedroom. Ten months later my mother was increasingly focused on giving birth to the lazy thing that lay complacently in her womb, four weeks overdue. Both of our two daughters would behave in the same way. My mother even tried running around a ploughed field to jog this child into action, but it was only backing the winner (of the Ladies' Race at the Fife Point to Point) that finally brought on labour. All the other riders had already fallen, and the crowd had gone mad, encouraging the one remaining rider (who was not the favourite) to complete the last round of fences. At 5.45 a.m. on 17 May 1960, **Barnaby Hugh Rogerson** came into the world. I was born at home (bleak-looking naval married quarters - harled against the wind, rain and neighbours) at 21 Somerville Road, Rosyth, Dunfermline. My father had developed jaundice on a cruise in the Far East and he had been grounded. The Navy wanted nothing to do with him. So my mother used him as a nursemaid for months - 'that was all he was good for, holding onto you, while he sat in an armchair' - while she looked after her two older children, Dido and David. Thus by happy chance I developed an easy physical relationship with my father, who at this stage of his naval career was often absent for years at a time.

I didn't need to ask my brother **James Francis Rogerson** for his birth story for I was there. James was born at home on 18 March 1964 in his parent's bed, but was nearly strangled by the umbilical cord which had wrapped itself around his neck. My father prayed to St Francis, but my mother gave the credit to Dr Ian Ruthven-Stuart, who unlooped the cord and remained an untouchable hero in her eyes thereafter. In later life Ian was also brave enough to look her in the eye and refuse to prescribe medication for her asthma whilst she continued to smoke so many cigars. James had a very happy infancy for he was fondly mothered by his older sister, so his two older brothers also liked him, and he was allowed to share our bedroom. Actually there was no choice once we had moved from Greengates in Denmead (a bungalow enclosed by a colonial-like verandah) to Waterside Cottage outside Soberton, which a kind relation

Barnaby Rogerson being tidied up by his father

described as a rural slum with an impeccable view. I remember James's first experience of schooling (in a nursery within the Naval College at Greenwhich) which was intense, so much so that when he came home we allowed him an hour as a dragon, running around on all fours, permitted to bite anyone he caught on the ground. Now, I believe, they have better ways to treat dyslexia. The other strong, early memory of James that I have is the happy way he had with animals, helping our mother with her chickens or a litter of basset puppies. He would also go into a contented trance the moment he was put on a horse. It was as if you had put the two parts of a centaur together, producing an incredibly easy and natural relationship between man and animal. It also suited my parents, who had both been brought up by horse-mad fathers, to have a child with a real 'seat'.

James's own memories begin with Virginia Beach, the unspeakable horrors of any schooling made even worse but not understanding a word they said. He always looked crushed coming off the yellow school bus, but then would sprint into life, playing games with our American neighbours (Jonathan Hurt and Mary Adler) and became a five-year old surf dude with his own waxed board, blond hair and a tan. Two and half years later, when he returned to England, he had become an American, and once again could not understand a word of what the teacher was saying. Then came Cottesmore, the Rogerson family boarding school, followed by Gordonstoun, which had a completely international, multi-cultural, mixed sex student body. James came alive for the sports (tennis, sailing, rugby), but lessons had to be endured – 'I just wanted to get through them and out the other side.' I was impressed when after the death of our mother we were clearing up my father's neat filing system of family papers. James found all his old school reports, and having briefly flicked through them, said 'clearly, they didn't think much of me then' and dropped them all into the fire. For a document-hoarding, book-collector, it was a shock but also a revelation. However, Gordonstoun had its good side, for there he Laura Rogge, his first German girlfriend. My mother had taken German lodgers in the summer holidays (from a local language school) and James and I were both permanently affected by this experience of living beside tall, self-possessed girls who combined beauty with seriousness.

James did not bother with the school cadet force and took life-saving classes on Findhorn beach instead, but once his two brothers had failed to get into the Navy and the Army, the military life beckoned as an option. He joined his maternal grandfather's regiment, the Queen's Own Hussars, in which his mother's cousin and her uncle had also served. He passed out of Sandhurst on a pair of crutches, his ankle and his knee broken playing rugby against the French army. A period in Catterick (the Royal Armoured Corps training ground) was followed by seven years guarding the German frontier based on Schloss Brederbeck, Bergen, Hohne. James qualified as an elite reconnaissance-troop leader, but in one exercise his 54-ton tank disappeared underwater. The cargo of explosive charges swelled with water and started bobbing around like party balloons. This was a bad thing. But James dived into the mud and rescued his driver which was considered a good thing. Years later I witnessed a form of this determination when one of his horses fell into a deep pool of silage, and in he went after her, keeping her head up 'otherwise she would have been gone'. There were also more glamorous activities, an inter-regimental polo tournament played in the 1936 Berlin Olympic Arena, playing rugby for the British Army, skiing for

James Francis Rogerson, Queens Own Hussars

his regiment, polo scholarships in New Zealand (which included training to be a blacksmith) and qualifying as a mountain leader, taking soldiers off to train in the wilds of Norway, Switzerland, Germany, Scotland and other places. He guarded the Maze prison in Northern Ireland for a period, which at first seemed like a horror story – 'you were pointing guns at your own people' but after a month it became disturbingly normal. He developed a respect for the intelligence service of the IRA, who, though imprisoned, would often achieve psychological mastery over their captors through disciplined observation, 'catching hold of any passing gossip and then probing to for any weakness in character amongst their guards'. After ten glorious years as a junior officer, James got married to his German girlfriend, Corinna Stahl in September 1993, and left the army that December. James did not want to become a staff officer. Corinna's father and grandfather had been colonels of German cavalry regiments, so she knew what to expect, in terms of sharing your life with horses and dogs and drinking Hoch like water. James's ability to sleep-walk (stark naked through the streets of Berlin) and return (having entered the door-code in his comatose state) revealed some of the differences between a British and a German cavalry officer.

Wedding of Corinna Stahl and James Rogerson

James had recognised that Corinna loved her work (she was a trained physiotherapist like his own mother) and it was he who would need to fit into Germany, and not for him to move his wife to England. James learned German. A German polo friend warned him, 'sure, we can all speak perfect English, most especially when we are selling to you, but if it is you who are trying to sell to us, then this has to happen in Deutsch.' James took whatever jobs he could get, in whatever German city. There was a year as the regional manager for three dozen multi-storey car parks, 'working for a total cunt, a rude, moody, unpleasant, bi-polar bastard", then eighteen months running a new shopping-residential development (Marzahan Centre) in old East Berlin. A friend from in his old regiment, Eric Popps, spotted an advertisement for an International Sales Manager for the Ambridge Group, a Telecom Consultancy. The only threat during the interview process came from a rival, Leo, but fortunately both were taken on. James worked a summer in Frankfurt then set up a branch for Ambridge in Switzerland. After a year James and Leo Kidel began to realise that their boss was a liability and took the bold decision to set up for themselves, in 1999.

They employ skilled engineers, who are constantly testing, expanding, mending, improving, suggesting and creating new forms of telecommunications. The task is to find a client who wants this team to do a task (they can do anything) but doesn't want the challenge of managing these boffin-engineers for themselves. It took James and Leo ten years to get the attention of the really important clients, who have lots of work that needs doing and who pay on time. There were some really tough years during this decade, when certain foreign companies did not pay their bills very quickly, and then decided to pay them in local currency that is not easily convertible. There was an even tougher time when the invoices had to be made out in euros, but the engineers liked to be paid in Swiss francs. Which was not a problem, unless the exchange rate moves quicker than the invoices are being settled at their dated conversion rate. And it was. Then they were tested by the dot.com bubble bursting (2003) and having just weathered that by the financial crisis unleashed by the collapse of Lehman brothers (September 2008). In 2012 they turned the corner. They now employ 950 people in Germany, England, Switzerland, Roumania, France, Denmark and Spain and turnover a hundred million.

My niece and nephew (Carlotta and Nicholas) were brought up in Switzerland, speak German at home, English in Germany and Swiss to their horses. When I last talked to them Carlotta was in the Swiss national team for dressage while learning to be a trainer and Nicholas was using his summer holiday (from Barcelona University) to play polo.

Father and Son, wearing the same number on their backs, so just exercising their polo ponies not playing as half a team

CHAPTER FOUR

Making the family skeleton dance: Three male role models

If you cannot get rid of the family skeleton, you may as well make it dance.
George Bernard Shaw

I was fortunate to have known my father and his two brothers (Barry Rogerson and Nico Rogerson) very well. They were a discordant but undeniably lively group of men. They had no friends in common, but were extremely fond of their cousins, so now and then the three of them would be assembled together for a marriage or a funeral or a wedding anniversary. All three men were obsessively punctual and believed in being immaculately turned out, once they stepped outside of their own garden. To guarantee a margin of error in order to be 'on time', they would arrange to meet before any actual event at an inn, in order

to celebrate their punctuality with a drink or two while keeping an eye on the clock. Looking back on them from the hindsight of my own old age, I can also now see that collectively they were a rather odd group of male role models, but they were all charismatic individuals who succeeded in forging a life of their own choice.

Barry Hugh Rogerson (1926-2006) was amusing, charming, brave and wicked. He was the elder son of Hugh Rogerson and Gertrude Rochford, born on 10 August 1926. The best part of his childhood was spent in Sacomebury Farmhouse in Hertfordshire, which backed on to its

Back yard of Sacombebury Farmhouse, with its own kennels and stables

Barry and Keith, Christmas 1937

*Barry and Keith as pageboys with their cousin Valda
in between, 1934*

Hugh Rogerson flanked by his two sons, 1938

own stable yard and was isolated within the grounds of Sacombe Park. His mother died when he was fourteen and was buried in the little isolated church at Sacombe. This tragedy coincided with the war and his father being called back into the Navy. So Barry spent a lot of time with the local gamekeeper, Len Hale who taught him to identify dozens of birds by their song alone.

Barry was educated at Worth Abbey and Downside. He was proud of both places. I can hear him explain that Eton was the Protestant version of Downside but my father later told me that Barry had not fitted in at either place. He was a loner. Barry was much happier in the Irish Guards in the last year of the war. A brother officer (Gerald Mount Eagle) recalled him as 'intrepid and fearless and daring. A regiment needs people like Barry. But not too many of them.' Uncle Barry was indeed an extreme character, though you would never guess it from his outward form. He was always well turned out in a finely tailored lightly woven tweed suit, with his gold watch chain hanging from a lapel, red and blue striped guards tie and perfectly polished shoes. But he was also a man capable of shooting a neighbour's

ginger cat (to protect a nesting thrush). Six-year-old Emma Rogerson heard her neighbour Mrs Gudgeon calling 'pussy, pussy.' She innocently apprised her of the truth, 'you won't find your cat, you know – because daddy shot it'. On another occasion, he was being chased by two police cars yet again drunk in charge of a car after the Derby races. Barry managed to reach his farmhouse first, and then rushed out to release Archer, a savage Alsatian dog, who hounded the young police officers back into their cars. Barry then poured himself a large whisky at his front door, raising his glass in a toast to the police cars in an attempt to invalidate any breath test.

He was a brilliant amateur jockey (like his father) and a total countryman who shot, hunted, sailed and could drink more than any man I have ever met, without slurring his words. Barry poured himself a tumbler of brandy and port last thing at night, which sat beside his bed, waiting to be the kick start to his morning. During the day he would sample several pints of local beer (which he considered part of his working day, keeping an eye on the quality of the local ale as a Maltster). He was also a self-appointed watchman of the English pub

Barry and Keith staying with Aunt Eileen and their cousin Valda

the Inn you continue to use !

McMULLEN'S

Brewers in Hertfordshire since the
Reign of George the Fourth

The money received for this race card will be treated as a subscription
to the General Funds of the Puckeridge Hunt.

PRICE 2/6   PRICE 2/6

THE PUCKERIDGE HUNT.

POINT-TO-POINT STEEPLECHASES

Subject to National Hunt Regulations for Point-to-Point Steeplechases

SATURDAY, MARCH 28th, 1953

WICKHAM HALL, Bishop's Stortford

(by kind permission of Frank Harvey, Esq. Junr., Vincent Routledge, Esq.
and F. M. Prime, Esq.)

Stewards:
Brig. E. H. L. Beddington, C.M.G., D.S.O., M.C.   *Tom Howard, Esq.
*H. Gingell, Esq.   *Cmdr. H. S. Rogerson, R.N.

* Acting Stewards.

Judges: | N. S. Pryor, Esq.
| Major T. E. Dimsdale, M.C.
Starter: Lt.-Col. R. L. Bristowe, T.D.
Asst. Starter: Cmdr. J. Herapath, R.N.
Hon. Clerks of Scales: | W. R. Kemsley, Esq.
| K. S. Holland, Esq.
Hon. Veterinary Surgeons: | A. Millar, Esq. M.R.C.V.S.
| L. Wakley, Esq. M.R.C.V.S.
Hon. Medical Officer: Dr. G. G. Holmes.
Saddling Ring Steward: Col. J. H. Dennis.
Hon. Farriers: | A. Rayment, Esq.
| W. Horsnell, Esq.
Announcer: Myles Routledge, Esq.
Number Board: Jim Butter, Esq.
Clerks of the Course and Hon. Secretaries: | T. T. Streeter
| G. Sparrow
15/15, North Street, Bishop's Stortford

All persons attending the meeting do so at their own risk. The Committee accept
no responsibility for damage to such persons or their property.

A Totalisator selling 2/-, 10/- and £1 Tickets for a " Win " only will be in operation,
staffed by the Racecourse Betting Control Board.

WARREN BROS. & COOKE, LTD., PRINTERS, ROYSTON, HERTS.

Racecard – from the day Barry won four races in one day, 28 March 1953

Barry Rogerson

in his neighbourhood and insisted that at an early age that we understood the differences.

An inn was a way-station that stood on the old coach and mail routes that bound England together, linking the centre of London with every market-town and port. So a pre-dawn four-in-th- morning start from the White Horse (where London's Ritz hotel now stands) gave you a meal halt at Alresford and took you to the docks of Southampton by dusk, matched by the coach route that stopped at Petersfield for a meal and change of horses before reaching the docks at Portsmouth. All over London there were such links. The Bull Inn in London's Leadenhall street was paired with the famous old Red Lion in Colchester. Barry taught us that an inn was the centre of every English town (often flanked by rivals linked to different coaches) and because it would be complete with a working courtyard for the change of horses, it had to be equipped with stables, hay and straw lofts, fresh water and the available skills of a local wheelwright and blacksmith. The middle of the eighteenth-century was the heyday of the coach, when over seventeen thousand vehicles

Barry riding Silver Grill, Towcester Races

were in operation, each with eight passengers snug inside and ten on the roof. The inn was the nail that held in place all these ribbons of trade and was able to provide meals and beds at all hours. In the old days, there were no numbered houses on our streets. Letters and goods would be sent to the local inn, where negotiations with carriers would start. Before the great era of the coach and four, England had been knit together by couriers (also known as carriers) who led caravans of pack-horses across the land. A pack-horse could carry a 250 lb load, and had the advantage of being able to cross fords and follow tracks, impossible for a coach which always had to pay its way at the tolls that guarded bridges and good roads.

A tavern was a notch or two down in scale from an inn but would be able to provide some choice of foreign wines and British spirits. An ale house was a much simpler affair, often run by a widow, serving just ale and beer in a front room. These three units were the heart of a community (be it a town-centre inn, a village tavern or the ale house that served just a street) where the beer had to be

charged for, but the welcome and the chat was free. The barrels would be delivered by the brewery in a dray pulled by horses. In the old days, wooden barrels of beer didn't like travelling very far, which effectively meant that beer was seldom drunk more than ten miles from the place it was brewed.

Before sitting down to Sunday lunch it was Barry's habit to start off with a lightly chilled bottle of hock while chatting as he watered his flowers and seedlings in a small but jungle rich conservatory. Wines, carefully selected to go with the food, flowed throughout the meal. Two days afloat with Barry on the *Ena*, the old red-sailed Thames sailing barge, would mix up tough old head brewers and representatives of the Beerage with step-sons and nephews on board to act as stewards. It was like sailing with a British Bacchus, with the gossip reaching back two hundred years. It was also a sad tale, revolving around the loss of skilled local employment. In 1954 there had been 450 family-owned breweries and maltsters across the land, but within twenty years they had been transformed into 'the big six' industrial breweries who advertised

Pair of Plough horses photographed during the War

nationally and dominated 80% of the trade. So the mood on the *Edna* would often dwell on the eighteenth and nineteenth heyday of British brewing. How the Quaker families never touched gin but could brew with pride, upholding 'temperance' but damning 'abstinence' as irrational. The Quakers avoided military service, the universities, the law and the clergy but married each other and looked after their own. So a Quaker family such as the Phillipses at Royston, not only ran their own brewery for 224 years but by intermarriage became shareholders of twenty-five other family breweries. The Anglican families of England's Beerage tended to be distracted from good business practices as their children were leeched away from trade into the professions. Barry told us about the Christie family who had employed his grandfather to run the great Hoddesdon Brewery which also distilled spirits. How the Christie's lost £3,000 pounds in a famous highway robbery (which happened in 1814), which would have been the annual turnover of a county brewery. There was always an association between money and beer. For it was an English fiscal tradition that it was much easier to collect duty from the maltsters (where the sacks of Malt could be weighed and assessed with ease over an eight-month season, October to May) than with the finished liquid made by the breweries and pubs, which could spill, be watered down, go off or leak in dozens of different ways. So the maltsters, not only made malt but became a vital cog in the collection of revenue. Duty would be assessed every six weeks. These were big sums, for the excise duty would be 45% of your turnover. The maltsters grew used to covering these costs with local bonds, giving them six months of credit. This provided an easy road into banking, as did buying the crops of barley from the farmers, or the raising of mortgages on ploughed land. So this was the path that led the Hoare family, as well as the Barclays (allied to a dozen other Quaker clans) from beer and malting into banking. The Christies were having a go at this when their stage coach was hit by highwaymen.

Without ever losing his temper, Barry could be exceptionally outspoken and direct with men (the large nose broken in the boxing ring gave notice of a man prepared to fight), but was never other than charming and attentive with women. My mother who grew up in the same part of Hertfordshire

remembered in her old age that he had good taste in women, and as a young man went out with Anne Fletcher and Felicity-Anne Baer who were both much brighter than him but liked his energy and delight in life. He was nominally a Roman Catholic but never attended church after they ended the Latin Mass. He could be witty but was not loud, allowing words to slip out through his stiff upper lip. My mother was always wary of him, worrying that he played himself up to be a rich-man's fool, a perennially popular guest on their yachts, at the races or at a shoot, but a big part of his job was to charm the brewers into buying his malt and so keep the business alive.

Barry Rogerson had a passionate commitment to his own neighbourhood. He held an alcoholic court of local opinion in the back bar of the Punch House on Friday evenings, which would champion the revival of the old open-air Tuesday market at Ware. He was supported by Mr Day, the green-grocer, in achieving this. They knew their local history - that the light, well-drained soils of east Hertfordshire produced some of the best barley in the world and that the triangle formed by Ware-Hoddesdon and Hertford had been making the best malt in England for at least five hundred years. Malt had been shipped down to London on barges on the river Lea since records began, which in this particular case was 1339. When McMullen's Brewery agreed to close the French Horn pub in Ware, the chairman sadly took the boardroom vote but then turned to his fellow directors and said, 'I don't know how I am going to face Barry.' The same concern was felt when the owners of Morrells Brewery in Oxford shut up shop, ending a long tradition of local employment in the heart of the city. Barry argued 'No-one shuts city-centre cathedral, a brewery is no less important.'

Barry loved his visits to local farmers, bargaining as they walked the fields (chatting and reminiscing) but always proud that at the end of the day, the ledger showed that he bought better barley and cheaper than Ipswich. He started working at Page and Harrington after he left the Irish Guards in 1948. It was a traditional malting house, one of twenty such family-owned businesses in Ware. My father remembered this old family malting business with bemused affection, especially a foundation stone that had been laid by great-grandfather Josiah

Rogerson. The head clerk wore a frock coat and wrote out bills with a steel nib at a standing desk. Great brick kilns lined with horse-hair were fired up with bundles of coppiced hornbeam 'which burns like a candle'. The barley seed would be spread out in the malting houses, usually made up of three storeys of chambers with six-foot-six high ceilings. Then it would be sprinkled with water for two to three days for the soaking. Then it would be spread out three to twelve inches deep for a fortnight, and then closely observed, so when the seed started to bud (three-quarters the length of the grain) it would be dried with blasts of hot air. Then the sprouted barely would be roasted (just like coffee) to give you the colour of your final beer, black for a porter or light amber for a pale ale. There was a whole spectrum of colours: Double stout, Oatmeal stout, Milk stout, Brown ale, Best Red ale, Light ale, Light bitter ale, Old ale, Luncheon ale, all the way down to Mild or Small, which throughout the first half of the nineteenth century would be provided to schools and workhouses in preference to contaminated drinking water. Hops were first added as a preservative (and only later did we take to the taste) with beer normally being rated as about half as strong as ale in alcohol. Teams of young workers, all dressed alike in caps, cotton trousers tied with string and canvas boots turned the malt over with wide ash-wood shovels. Old men were given the simpler task of filling and sewing up the hessian sacks by hand before snoozing away the afternoon. For there was a flowing 'tap' on hand from the brewery to cool down the workers, whose shifts started at dawn, and who worked on into the night in the season. Business was either done in the saddle, meeting farmers on their own land out hunting, or at the table, wining and dining the brewers of London and East Anglia.

After the war, Barry went on a tour of German breweries and maltings, in order to understand what changes were needed to keep a family business thriving. But he could never convince his father to invest in the new machinery, though the Commander was always good for another hunter or a risk on a race-horse. The malting business was always more of a hobby than a passion, and while his father lived at Reed Hall, he also dabbled as a farmer.

Barry fell out with his stepmother, who was possibly jealous of the close relationship between father and son. Her own son, Nico, would be good at most sports but lacked the one thing that his father valued, which was a good seat on a horse. Things got even more complicated when Barry fell in love with Peggy Page-Croft, the vivacious wife of his father's business partner, Richard Page-Croft. Peggy had style. Her father was an Argentine architect. Things had first become apparent after Peggy had called, 'light me up Darling' at a drinks party and two men had advanced to light her cigarette.

There had been a promising amalgamation of local family businesses in 1962 when J.R.Page of Bishops Stortford, J.Harrington of Hertford and Henry Ward of Ware all came together. But in 1965 this local grouping sold out to Pauls of Ipswich. Barry stayed on, determined loyally to work with the new proprietors. Fortunately he had retired before the Ware works were closed in 1994. Barry later had the satisfaction of watching Hugo Page-Croft, his stepson, do what he had wanted to do and succeed very well with it. Moray Maltings in the Scottish Highlands became an astonishingly successful business. Barry had proved himself an exceptionally jolly step-father to Hugo, Ricky and Dawn Page-Croft. Despite the divorce, he and Peggy ended up occupying an isolated farmhouse (Noahs Ark Farm) on the Fanhams Hall estate of the Page-Croft family. His daughter, my cousin Emma Rogerson, was a jolly, warm-hearted country girl, but though she had plenty of lovers, she never settled down to have children of her own. A few years after she buried her old father, she was found drowned in a pond. She might have slipped when going out for a walk after midnight, but I know how she missed her father, whom she once praised as even better company than a dog.

Years before he died Barry had made a list of all his cherished possessions and carefully divided them up among his surviving relations. So we each found a note in his hand pinned to the back of a picture, a wooden malting shovel or a pair of silver cups. Barry had left me two pictures. A landscape of some Hertfordshire fields which had been given to Barry by the artist, when he was a lonely, lost boy. For after his mother died Barry used to spend hours watching Walter Fletcher working on his canvasses, wrapped up in an outdoor cape. Walter was their neighbour who owned Saccombe Park. He was a large and imposing figure of a man, the son of a

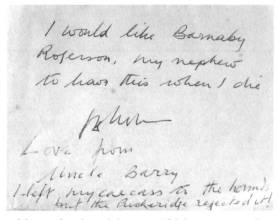

Message from beyond the grave, " I left my carcass to the hounds but the Puckeridge rejected it"

baron of the Austro-Hungarian Empire (Fleischl von Marxow) who had renounced this identity to become a plain-speaking English gentleman. Walter had been sent to Charterhouse and then as a young man fought against the German army in East Africa during the First World War. Walter Fletcher's family ran the Hecht, Levis and Kahn trading group which did its best to dominate the world rubber market. During the Second World War Walter ran an immensely profitable smuggling division for the SOE, after which he became a conservative M.P. and was knighted for his various services. Walter was locked into a tempestuous relationship with a Scottish opera singer. Both my father and Barry remember listening to Neville Chamberlain declare war in the drawing room of Saccombe Park set against a live rendition of 'The Skye Boat Song' sung by Esme Boyd. She would eventually agree to become Lady Fletcher. My other inheritance was a portrait of a foxhound painted by Richard Barrett Davis (a local painter from Hertfordshire) who was the son of King George III's private huntsman of harriers. There was a footnote: 'I left my carcass to the hounds but the Puckeridge [his local hunt] rejected it! Love from Uncle Barry.'

Nico Rogerson (1943-2017) was a card-player, a risk-taker, a brilliant shot, a passionate fisherman, an inspired cook and an attentive host. He had a quick wit but one that was tempered by his natural charm and kindness. I cannot recall an angry word - though he had eloquent hand gestures with which he could deliver a judgement. Nico was always active, as close to Peter Pan as any mortal I

have met. He lived life to the full, wonderfully alive to the moment, and forever charmed by the prospect of the next adventure. He was highly intelligent but not the least bit interested in matters of the soul or the spirit, in self-examination or introspection. He was fascinated and generous with this life but was indifferent to any promise of the next. He whispered to my younger brother just two days before he died, 'Game Over'.

Over a memorably liquid twenty-four hour train journey to meet my brother James in the Alps I had the time to question my uncle about his childhood. Nico was born in the middle of the war when his father was serving in the Royal Navy. He and his young mother had to take refuge with a whole clan of Rogersons sheltering in his grandfather's house, Red Court. After the war he was brought up in Reed Hall, Royston, Hertfordshire. Nico saw his father Hugh Rogerson as a distant and authoritarian figure, who had by that time served in two world wars. Nico was aware that he had been wounded in a gun turret as a young midshipman at the Battle of Jutland, and knew he was obsessed with horses, hounds, hunting and racing. Commander Hugh Rogerson preferred the company of his eldest son Barry, who was not only a successful amateur jockey but worked beside him at Harrington & Page.

In this environment Nico forged a very close bond with his mother, Olivia Worthington, while his boarding schools (Cheam followed by Winchester) were more of a liberation than a tribulation, and according to Nico were chosen by his father due to their proximity to the Newbury racecourse. In the holidays Olivia had the good sense to take him to the bustling households of his hospitable Rogerson uncles, either to Cottesmore with its own grass tennis courts and golf course, animated by his playmate cousins Mary-Lou, Mark and Mathew or to his uncle John, to be included in the shoots in Sussex and Norfolk. Whenever I questioned Nico about his father, I noticed how he first instinctively checked that his shoes were polished and his finger-nails were clean before answering carefully. But, now they are both gone, I see not what kept them apart, but what they shared: a lifelong horror of a stained shirt or of being late, and a delight in fast cars and women. Aside from his three wives, I remember stumbling across traces of other girlfriends Nico had had as a student: Chantal from Belgium vastly improved

Nico Rogerson with childhood companions

Nico as a schoolboy

Nico whilst sailing across the Pacific

his French, his German was upgraded by Christina from Strasbourg and Sandra from *Vogue* sharpened his aesthetic eye.

He learned many languages (and the ways of the world) by working as a tour guide on Thompson coach tours round Europe during his year off. He studied Law at Magdalene College, Cambridge (1962-5) at his father's insistence. After graduating in 1965 Nico worked for the *Financial Times*. This was the time when he got to know the Elliot family: George, Ian and Alan, who was already emerging as something big in the City but kept things lively in the evening by running an illegal chemin-de-fer table in Belgrave Square. Nico could sing, dance and play every game known to man (including real-tennis) with a cheerful zest and a love of the game, but you had to watch your wallet, and the doubling dice, once the backgammon board was opened.

Four years after leaving university, in 1969, he set up Dewe-Rogerson with Roddy Dewe. The two had met by chance at a fashionable tailor's shop. Nico was already fascinated by the inner workings of the City of London. Dewe-Rogerson directed the financial PR campaign which sold off British Gas so successfully (the 'Tell Sid' campaign which stimulated a perception of scarcity) that they later advised the government on the sale of Britoil, TSB, BP, British Steel and the water and electricity monopolies. Dewe-Rogerson could claim to have spearheaded the Thatcherite revolution which created the post-socialist world order, though the initial promise of a new share-owning democracy did not emerge. By 1988 Dewe-Rogerson were turning over 70 million pounds worth of business and employing 400 of the best and brightest. Nico established branches in New York, Central Europe and the Far East to create a worldwide brand which in 1998 was sold for 27 million pounds. He stayed on for a year to oversee the merger with Citigate, after which he devoted his talents to enjoying life as well as setting up a consultancy, 'Concept to Profit.' AIGIS Blast Protection was one of the companies Nico invested in, which briefly threatened to create a second fortune for him, after demand for blast-proof secure containers spiralled in the wake of 9/11.

The thing I admired about him most, was his loyalty to his old friends, especially when they were in need. As well as knowing many of the most exalted

The board of Dewe-Rogerson, a homage to the cover album of Breakfast in America, top from left Tony Carlisle and David Pollock, lower from left, Nico, Roddy Dewe in centre, then Johnny de Uphaugh

people across the globe, he also had an infectious delight in a rogue and a lygger, a chancer out of luck but still showing some pluck. Tales about Paddy Pakenham spring instantly to mind. The oldest core of Nico's many circles of friends was the 'ice-cream set' (David Enderman, Andrew Rayner and David Tonge) who found each other at Cambridge in 1962. It was very difficult for any foreigner to feel welcomed by an Englishman at that time (and probably still is). But if you talked to Renji Sathiah, later a Malay diplomat, Farid Khoury, a Lebanese lawyer, George Hyatt from Palestine, or Persian's such as Khosrow Shahabi or Parvis Khozeimeh-Alam, or Boulas Sara still trading out of Damascus, or Sebastian Santa Cruz from Chile they can explain how truly exceptional Nico was as a young man. He was not only untouched by a flicker of racial prejudice, but delighted in knowing their family stories, their culture and style. These were real friendships, full of laughter and shared misadventures, young men drawn together by the intoxicating fun of gambling, nightclubs and the lure of the perfect lunch. One of them described Nico as a Greek God with the manners of an English gentleman. An e-mail sent to me by Andrew Rayner gives us a taste of this era:

> After a week's skinful of vino de Jerez celebrating the autumn sherry harvest-home, the *Vendimia*, we climbed into my tiny Piper and flew off across Andalucia, on the way buzzing Fermin Bohorquez's bull ranch, Nico hanging out to drop a beach ball inscribed with lipstick into a bullring where we had the day before been fighting his young bulls at a *tienta*. We flew *up* the rock wall of Arcos de la Frontera to surprise friends with a house right on the edge. A day or two with friends in Malaga, then, filing a flight plan to Morocco as one had to in those days of Spanish blockade, we headed for Gibraltar, landing on that remarkable runway across the isthmus and the only road into the Rock, with sea at both ends. I don't think either of us was sober till after we arrived in Rabat, a full week after leaving Jerez and the entertainments of the generous Domecq family. Yet all this time Nico was a relaxed conspirator, somehow trusting in fate to preserve him from the mistreatment of a sherry-sodden pilot, laughing all the while and taking the controls from time to time. A few days thereafter we picked up Renji, an old Cambridge friend, now a third secretary at the Malaysian Embassy in Morocco, and his girlfriend to fly through the High Atlas mountains to the desert. All was well until we tried to take off from Ouarzazate to fly back to Marrakesh, forgetting that the high and thin Saharan air didn't hold little aeroplanes up as well as conditions at sea level. By this stage we were also a bit overloaded with women. By heaving on the flaps we got off the ground in time to avoid the valley at the end of the sand runway, then bounced off dunes for a kilometre or two before staggering into the air.

To his young nephews and niece, Uncle Nico was the very spirit of adventure and self-confidence. My older sister Dido happily confessed that in her dreams he was always muddled up with rock stars. The contrast with our parents, dutifully scrimping away in their characterful but small dark Hampshire cottage to pack us off to boarding schools on a naval officer's salary, was always intriguing. Nico lived in the heart of glamorous London, and we got to witness this life as his door was always open to us, as we commuted between boarding schools and foreign naval bases. The flat in Sussex Gardens (rather over-filled with all his father's silver racing cups) was followed by a Barbican apartment right around the corner from the Dewe-Rogerson office on London Wall, then he went west to Chelsea, 61 Oakley Gardens followed by 32 Rossetti Garden Mansions, in due course upgraded to a large townhouse at 12 Redcliffe Road, then a mews cottage in Redan Street (side by side with his new father-in-law) and from thence to Bramham Gardens.

As an impressionable teenager I remember his drawing room in St Loo Avenue strewn with invitation cards. There was a series of erotic Beardsley prints hung in the corridor and on the other side of the wall a series about a Regency buck flirting and gambling and trying to escape his creditors. One learned early on to take the evenings as they unfolded. On one occasion, I watched as Nico's redoubtable old mother was given last-minute instructions to act as hostess for a drinks party they were throwing, because that highly desirable couple Mr and Mrs Nico Rogerson had decided to go elsewhere. But in the mornings, Nico was always uncle in charge, double checking our flights as he cooked a dawn breakfast, and always driving us himself (very fast, very skilfully, knowing the hourly shifts in London traffic flow as well as any cabbie) and using the time in the car to have that proper talk. This became the accepted pattern of our relationship, as decades of Rogerson marriages, funerals and celebrations threw us together for missions which would involve hampers and checking out restaurants *en route*. Nico was even closer to my younger brother James, who is a mirror image of his uncle in his passion for skiing, shooting and life in the fast lane.

I was lucky to have known and loved the very different characters of all three of my aunts: Elizabeth Rummel, Caroline Le Bas and Dinah Verry. Nico blamed himself for the break-up of his first marriage, which happened during the years he spent building up the international division of Dewe-Rogerson. In their heyday, they were a beautiful couple, and Elizabeth remained a model who also dabbled in fashion and design. Her father was a Polish professor who taught mechanical engineering and studied the evolution of the gun turrets of the Royal Navy as a hobby. Nico was a loving and generous stepfather to Elizabeth's two sons, Michael and Sandy, who would both add Rogerson to their Polish surname. He entered their lives on Christmas Day in 1972 when they eight and eleven years old. They were immediately enchanted by this man who took them for a drive in his open-top Porsche wearing a leather jacket and singing as he drove at incredible speeds.

Caroline Le Bas ran her own PR company which worked with Dewe-Rogerson but that never got in the way of her passionate commitment to the Labour Party which she shared with her father, Lord Gilbert. She would later use her skills to develop Philip Gould's focus groups, with the help of which Tony Blair seized control of the middle ground of politics. It was Caroline's passion for sailing that took them across the Pacific and first brought Nico to the Isle of Wight. They initially rented a simple terraced house in Yarmouth (2, Coastguard cottage) before they found a house that overlooked Newtown Creek. Her early death nearly felled the otherwise unquenchable optimism of Nico.

But very fortunately, Nico found Dinah. She was as clever and as good a cook as he was and had also sadly buried the love of her life. She knew all about the Rogerson family but in a good way. Her uncle Tim Nicolson had married Valda Rogerson, Nico's first cousin. For fifteen happy years, Nico and Dinah Rogerson turned the Old Parsonage above Newton Creek in the Isle of Wight into a place of legendary and abundant hospitality for their friends and for their extended families.

My father, **Keith Frank Rogerson** (1928-2004) was a naval officer and a Hampshire County Councillor who served God and his country. He was a Tory of the old 'one nation' school, who believed in service and the importance of family, church and community. He revered the Queen and the Pope but instinctively distrusted just about everyone else.

He cut a distinctive figure with his great Punch-like nose, the glow of health on his red cheeks and a pair of enormous shaggy eyebrows which veiled his bright-blue enquiring eyes. I can see him now tending to his evening tasks, bending down in the late-afternoon light to fill a watering-can at the River Meon's edge, then leaning over the fence to look at his livestock and check on the chickens before returning to feed his dogs and then, with a twinkle in his eye, to pour himself and my mother a glass of whisky.

My father never showed any aptitude for making money, or even for that matter bargaining with what he had, whether he was buying a hunter, a second-hand speedboat in the Highlands or a teapot in Morocco. When he was thrifty it was always for the sound reason that he was currently short of funds – for like his father before him he was by nature a spender. I remember the time after years of home-brew improved upon by buying gut-rot wine from a hose-pipe down by the Gibraltar docks when the cheque from a family legacy finally came in. A week later he was near-drowning his hundred new friends in Gibraltar in vintage Taittinger champagne. For alongside such upright heroes as Nelson he also delighted in those hopeless Hanoverian dukes and regency dandies who could wager 'all Lombard street to a China orange'.

My father loved a good party. He certainly knew how to give one. 'One sour, two sweet, four strong, eight week' was his mantra for making a

Keith as a schoolboy

Cadet Keith Rogerson, Christmas 1942

punch or a cocktail. Indeed some of his parties were so good that they were also near disasters. I remember my parents' leaving party at Gibraltar, when the Governor-General had to be carried down the stairs of the garrison library. He was good company: witty, clever and funny, but he could also be fantastically indiscreet, devastatingly critical and dearly loved an argument. Everything was up for debate though each inch was fought over with no quarter offered or expected. Despite his love for the good things in life he also prided himself on his self-sufficiency – cleaning his own drains, growing his own vegetables, building his own boat and splitting his own logs. Aside from the odd night on the town for the ballet or a dinner, urban life held no real attraction for him. For he was a countryman through and through, a man who could name the stars on a midnight walk, identify birds from their flight and wild shrubs from their blossoms. He was at his most gentle when handling some injured animal, calming a frightened horse, inspecting the torn coat of a wounded dog or stroking a frightened chicken that had been half-mauled to death by a fox.

He had an instinctive passion for plants and a love of gardens and gardening. As well as at Waterside Cottage, I remember the energy he threw into making gardens elsewhere, like on the back terrace of Scud Hill in Gibraltar, full knowing that in two years he would move on. He was generous with his energy. On our family camping trips, whether in some deserted cove on the Yugoslav coast or in an American wilderness, he was always proud to leave the place looking in better shape than when we arrived. At Virginia Beach he organised all the local kids into clearing the dunes of rusting metal cans by paying them a nickel a tin. Typically he then went rather over the top by making a large pyramid from these cans in the front yard, and hoisting an eighteenth century colonial flag with a notice attached that the British had at last returned to clean up America. He was not however to be numbered amongst the 'Neat-Pots' and was always a 'Shambler' – one who allowed weeds their place in a garden and preferred a muddy track to a tarmac path.

Though physically strong, he was a determined anti-sportsman all the days of his life, strenuously

Dad in pony trap

Barnes, Dad and Mike, motor torpedo boat

avoiding all team games and anything that involved a moving, spherical object. His interests were exclusively directed towards horses and hounds, whether hunting as a young man alongside his brother Barry, his elegant stepmother Olivia and his father the Field-Master or in later life by race-going and fence judging. Dogs were not considered companions they were his real friends, as deserving of affection, concern and proximity as any mere human. All his children were brought up amid a sea of bassets, my brother James was very nearly born with one on the bed. They would sleep on our pillows, wriggle their way into all the best seats of the sofa and drink from our bath water. On all the most important family occasions they would escape and for hours the surrounding woods would be filled with bellowing calls and the cracking of whips – and we would yet again be the family who turned up four hours late for an appointment. Three generations of home-bred bassets later – and with Juno consigned to the sea with full naval honours in Gibraltar harbour – came the momentous shift in loyalty to bloodhounds.

The half-insane Kimberley, who would claw her way through a dining-room wall in Kyle of Lochalsh, trash the interior of an Admiralty car and leap over walls to assault motorcyclists, yet proved herself to be an excellent tracker – and was the apple of my father's eye. She saved my brother David, then recovering from a broken back, when the house at Balmacara caught fire. Two further generations of bloodhounds (with Liberty and Jollity staying on at home) delighted him with manhunts organised over the hills of Wester Ross and the downlands of Hampshire. Friends of his children and hung-over cousins who had stayed the night, all made good prey. Then, to the secret relief of his friends, the decade of bloodhound slobber gave way to his daughter Dido's inspired gift of Gracie – a coal-black lurcher puppy from travellers on the west Coast of Ireland. A litter of puppies later saw the arrival of the mad but devoted Billy, a superb brindle matching pair to Black Boy, and the seventy-year old Commander was now equipped with just four dogs to control with his customary tangle of leads, whistles and hunting crops. This pack of lurchers added just the right level of anarchy and excitement to my father's expeditions along the Meon Valley, as well as terrorising the local wildlife. But as I overheard the old Droxford postman once observe,

'Alls well with the world, there goes the Commander out for a shout with his dogs.'

My father loved the sea, was indeed a natural seaman who never felt seasick and was intensely proud to have been a navigating officer in the Royal Navy – a job that we children thought the most important in the world. For it was Dad who got to hold the sextant, to take star sightings, to plot the course of the ship and to mark up the charts, to observe the winds, tides, dangerous headlands and shifting sandbanks. We loved the stories he brought back, as well as the presents and the hand-drawn birthday cards sent back from exotic places. In ships such as HMS *Morecambe Bay*, HMS *Crane*, HMS *Puma*, HMS *Vigo*, HMS *Cochrane*, HMS *Trafalgar* and the great aircraft carrier HMS *Eagle* he sailed the seven seas helping keep the Pax Britannica over the worlds sea-lanes. There were some great commissions, such as when his friends Sir Peter Troubridge and Tommy Sligo-Young all commanded their own motor torpedo boats - a flash flotilla of half a dozen high speed boats that were in and out of the Baltic between 1950 and 1952. Then he was given the job of racing *Marabu* – Hermann Goering's old yacht - under Sam Brooks's command across 1,400 miles of the Atlantic in the Newport to Bermuda race, leaving England on 31 March 1952 and getting a heroic welcome in the flesh-pots of the post-war Carribean from July 24th. But there were also the occasional horrors, of being struck by jet-launched rockets in the Red Sea and, as a midshipman, fishing up dead bodies blown up by mines in the Straits of Corfu.

Our favourite story was always 'muffle your oars' – an incident set during the Korean War and the Malaysian Emergency – where a brave detachment of marines had set off on their covert operation into the enemy-controlled coast with whispered instructions to muffle their oars with sacks. This they did, but by tying the sacks to the blades of the oars and not – as they should have – to their rollocks which created an extraordinary effect as they splished and sploshed their way across the sea.

I recently came across a note written by my father, where he seems to be sketching out a memoir of his youth at Dartmouth Naval College. The headings, 'sadistic staff, gun drill, mast climbing, punishments, coalmine, cadet revolt' tell their own

Motor torpedo boat squadron patrolling the Baltic in the Cold War

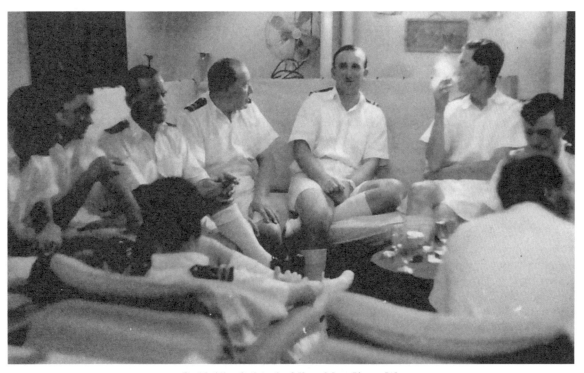

Dad holding forth in the Officers Mess, Korean War

*Mum and Dad on board the Royal Yacht,
when berthed in Gibraltar*

story. Fortunately, following an early attempt to destroy the whole college of cadets with a targeted airstrike, they were sent north. They occupied Eton Hall, one of the houses of the Duke of Westminster, among other places. As the submarine war progressed all able-bodied officers were needed for active service, so it was their good fortune to be taught by professors brought out of retirement, whom my father remembered as being both kind, inspiring and intelligent. He was also proud that it was his term that decided to stop the habitual bullying of the junior cadets, which he put down to the fact that they had a saint among them. Jean Vanier (the founder of the L'Arche communities) was first trained as a naval officer, and like Dad was a Roman Catholic. The other inspiring friendship from this period of his life was with Robert McCrum, an imposing giant of man whom we could never quite imagine fitting within the submarines that he would later command. Bobbie was a humanist and was diametrically opposed to my father politically, but their passionate arguments served only to strengthen their lifelong friendship. Though enchanted by the sea, Dad was not, I think,

a natural cog within any system. When they shared a cabin together, Andrew Waugh told how my father used to 'lose' a portion of the paperwork by filing it into a crack he had opened up in the metal bulkhead.

My father's last three jobs in the Navy – Commander of the Barracks in Portsmouth, Queen's Harbour Master in Gibraltar and then running BUTEC (the scientific research station in Kyle of Lochalsh which was trying to develop a drone-like intelligent torpedo) – were not at the sharp end of Ministry of Defence planning in Whitehall, but he enjoyed every minute of his command over these three little kingdoms, chatting dock hands out of strike action, quietly cleaning up corrupt practices, as well as running a newspaper, an eighteenth century library, with helicopter taxis and an elegant launch at his disposal.

Leaving the Navy was good for him, especially his brief career as a salesman, trying to sell 'Isle of Wight Cider', a murky, alcoholic brew, to a few tough-minded independent shopkeepers before the whole enterprise collapsed. The contrast with his grandfather Frank, who made a fortune from brewing beer in south London, provided much self-critical mirth. During this period my father also raised money for the Winged Fellowship charity by organising concerts in Winchester Cathedral, and worked beside two old colleagues, Admiral Colin McMullen and Admiral Alec Weir, as a marine consultancy. The three of them saved beaches, unblocked harbours, mended bridges and surveyed new anchorages in Devon, along the Thames, in St Lucia as well as designing a safe mooring for the historic ironship HMS *Warrior* back home in Portsmouth. After one long evening of marine consultancy at their office in London, he returned to find himself selected as the Conservative candidate for the Meon valley. He loved campaigning and hearing the real voice of the valley, not that all the requests he listened to, such as 'a few less of those uppity ladies on horseback' or 'you can let in the Jacobites for all I care' could be actioned. He also loved the public squabbles over planning, education and police budgets. He was very proud to have been an integral part of the campaign to save Droxford village school from closure from bureaucrats with 'eyes like tills and a heart like a cash register'.

In the last fifteen years of his life – with funds once again refreshed by a second family legacy – he became a relentlessly keen traveller, happily burdened like the navigator that he always was, with maps and schedules and keeping a keen eye on the prevailing wind direction. With his daughter working as a homeopath in the Burren Mountains (in Co Clare, Ireland), a son mapping the gold mines of South Africa and then surveying the jungles of Venezuela, another son exploring North Africa and his youngest son, a polo-playing cavalry officer turned techno-entrepreneur based in Germany and Switzerland, there was plenty of occasions, as well as the opportunity to travel. These twice-yearly journeys to catch up on the grandchildren always contained an element of near farcical disaster, but nothing, like being mugged in Caracas, nor a cliff fall in Ireland, nor childbirth in a Swiss blizzard, nor a bomb threat on the rail journey to St Petersburg, diminished the joy of these expeditions. Once, having survived yet another near-death experience whilst travelling with my parents (we were isolated in an islet on a wadhi besieged by the roaring waters of a flash flood in the Sahara) I asked him the closest he had ever come to the grave. He told me then about how he had taken a ship through a week-long Arctic storm (so violent that they could only head on north farther into the weather) on a near empty fuel tank without letting the rest of the crew realise the extent of their peril.

'What did you do then? I asked.

'Oh, I just carried on and tried to look confident', he replied.

It was this sort of discipline and self-control that he would later use in his two-year battle against his cancer, executed with magnificent sangfroid and a complete lack of self-pity. His campaign was so successful that many friends did not even know that he was ill, let alone dying. Only a fortnight before his death – at a time when he could hold down neither food nor drink and when he had very, very little strength left in his legs – he managed not only to get himself dressed up for the opera but to return entranced by the music.

But to truly understand my father you have to know that he had only one real passion in his life, one which gave him all the self-confidence, love and humour that he needed. When he stood beside my mother he always looked like the cat that got the cream. It was a love affair that had begun as a boy – for they were in the same pony club and their fathers, Major John Harvie and Commander Hugh Rogerson, both hunted together with the Puckeridge and Thurlow. This love took him through the whole voyage of his life. He used to declare that without my mother he would have become a Benedictine. 'You would have made a very bad monk', was my mother's habitual reply.

Towards the end of his life, my father decided to write down some of his childhood memories, which I have recently discovered.

"It's August 1939 on holiday with Mother and Father in a rented house near the beach at Frinton. A telegram arrives in the morning calling Father back into the Navy in September. Vivid memories of that breakfast, on a rabbit-grazed lawn, eating cream on grape nuts, a traditional holiday treat. Mother puts her hands to her cheeks and says, 'Oh Hugh'. Vague memories of returning home, then autumn term at prep school. Christmas holidays were very muted. Father's horses also called up for the war, which has now started, as well as his big Packard car – memories of a last 100 mph drive on the Newmarket road,

"We lived in a substantial farmhouse at Sacombe with dogs, ponies and bantams, a life we all loved. There was father's rather strange old groom Jack (who would fine us a packet of woodbines every time we fell off). Violet the cook, who had been caught on the kitchen table with Bowcock the handyman on a hot summer's day, and couples from time to time for semi-butlering and housekeeping.

"Easter holiday, 1940, mother caught pneumonia. Vivid memory of leaving her ill in bed with fantail pigeons on the window sill, she looking so pale and tired. Our adored vivacious and delightfully disorganised mother always our ally. Father tremendously admired but held in awe. Off to prep school. An afternoon in late April 1940 a prefect said, 'go to the headmaster at once he wants to see you.' Terrible dread, but nothing so bad as what was to come. My brother Barry already there looking pale and worried, past interviews in mind. The Headmaster, a kind man: 'I have to tell you that your mother died this morning. Your father will ring on the telephone in a few minutes. I'll leave you two here. God bless you.' Mind has gone a blank, vague memories of going to chapel and weeping, weeping, weeping everywhere.

"Somehow we discovered, though I do not remember how, that the house at Sacombe was to be let, our ponies taken to Aunt Eileen in Sussex and we were to go and live with our grandparents at Red Court, Haslemere, Surrey, where also was living our Aunt Eve and her husband Sandy, and Aunt Eve would help look after us.

"Red Court was already a place of dread because of previous Christmas visits – now it was to be our home. Vivid memory of turning into huge gates past the lodge down a long winding drive flanked by iron railings, through an entrance guarded by huge pillars surmounted by lanterns and into the large entrance hall – memory then fades, from misery, I suppose. Vaguer memories of a first night in unbelievably luxurious beds in a vast and over-furnished room.

"Red Court was a large red-brick mansion standing in 100 acres of garden, woods and park land. There were cottages, stables, garages, kennels, a huge greenhouse and lots of servants. A butler Charles, and an under-butler Bone (no Christian name for him), a parlour maid Ida, a chauffeur Reynolds, Mrs Graham the cook, with various kitchen and scullery maids coming and going. An upstairs maid Mrs Bone – very motherly. Outside there was the head gardener Mr Burton and two gardeners called Gauntlett, presumably brothers. These were gradually depleted by conscription, down to Ida, Reynolds, Mrs Graham and Mr Burton plus one Gauntlett. I mention these people behind the green baize door because they all became our best friends. Red Court was the third large house that my grandfather had owned, he moved about every seven years, and this was the grandest. The war prevented the next move.

"Grandfather was the seventh son of a Hertfordshire brewer and by the time we went to live with him he must have been a millionaire; which he achieved entirely through his own efforts and by fair means or foul. He had managed the Hammerton Brewery in Stockwell which brewed the nationally known Oatmeal Stout. One of his advertising campaigns 'Hammerton's Oatmeal Stout is as good as mother's milk' had been blazoned on London buses but had to be withdrawn after objections from the British Medical Association. He was also a senior member of the board of Eagle Star Insurance and involved in Lloyds. Despite all this he was a lovely man and always great fun for us to be with – but he was not there very much. Grandmother was always there.

"On the ground floor there was a dining room to the right of the hall, the green-baize door straight ahead, and then heading off the long end of an L-shaped hall – turn left to the drawing room – **Not** for children: then an imposing staircase and the morning room, Grandmother's lair – Not for children. At the end was a huge but lovely oak-pannelled room that doubled as a library. Children were allowed in and we loved that room. There was a huge radio-gram where we assembled for the nine o'clock news every evening before bed. We all stood up for the National Anthem at the end. Grandfather, after lots of squeaks and whistles, would sometimes get Lord Haw-Haw for he had an interminably inquisitive mind, even for the lies of Nazi propaganda. Grandmother, 'Frank must you listen to that awful man? I think it's most unpatriotic of you.' She was, as with most of her complaints to him, wasting her breath.

"Upstairs: leading off a large central landing and turning left was the Blue Room – ours; and beyond was Aunt Eve's suite of sitting room, bedroom, dressing room and bathroom, children very welcome. We loved her for herself and her eccentricities. To the left was a similar suite for our grandparents and beyond that the best guest room – the yellow room, later to be the subject of a family feud. Down a passage were two or three more bedrooms and a couple of bathrooms. A rhyme on the wall of ours told us

Always remember don't forget
Never leave the bath room wet
To leave the bath room full of water
That's a thing you never ought'er

Beyond the bathrooms was a back staircase coming up from the servants quarters to the bedrooms up on the second floor. There was a bit of a warren of rooms up there, which were later to be a great tribulation to Grandmother, who as a result was laid open to accommodating 'billetees' – English refugees escaping from the London Blitz. It's hard to say who suffered more in the end, Grandmother or the unfortunate people who were billeted on her.

"There were three other occupants of the house – 'Gillie' a little white Scottish terrier, and 'Poppet'

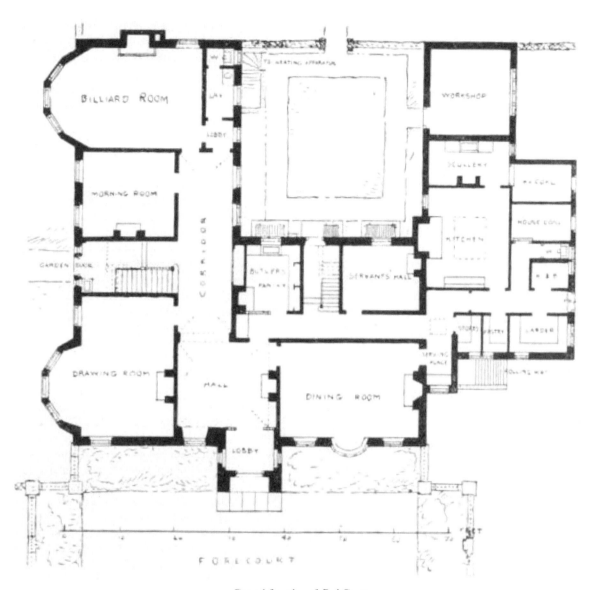

Ground floorplan of Red Court

a black terrier. In the conservatory leading off from the oak room in an imposing cage was a large and autocratic parrot called Laura. When the phone rang Luara would call out very clearly,

'Michael – telephone !'

Michael was Grandmother's youngest son and our uncle. Grandmother had got used to most of the telephone calls being for him, hence the call that Laura mimicked. We tried, in later years, to get Luara to swear abominably to shock Grandmother, but she didn't take to it. I have an early memory of playing on the floor with the terriers and hearing Grandmother loudly request advice on the telephone from a doctor. Was it normal for children to play on the floor with dogs or should she prevent this? As the evening drew in, we got up to pull the curtains but were stopped by Grandmother; 'leave those alone, that's the parlour maid's job.' Meals were very formal and always 'on time'. Luncheon and dinner were served by Charles and Ida. The latter would whisper in our ear which implement to use. Grandfather liked us to drink beer and port at a rather early age, so we rather enjoyed dinner – except one. At Christmas 1940, Grandfather, who liked to make a short speech, ended up with a toast 'to absent friends an especially our beloved Gertie'. This mention of my mother was too much for me and I had to be taken away because I could not (or would not) stop crying. Grandfather, who had loved our Mother almost more than his own daughters, understood. He never mentioned her again. Besides Grandparents, ourselves, Aunt Eve and Uncle Sandy there was a constant to-ing and throw-ing of other members of the family: Michael and Marion (youngest son and his wife); Betty (youngest daughter) whose husband Patrick Milligan served throughout the war in the Middle East; Kenneth Allenby (Grandmother's orphaned nephew), Jimmy Rock (Father's cousin) – so dinners were often large affairs with space for visiting friends as well.

"Sometimes after lunch Grandfather would play the grand piano in the drawing room. He would play the Cockney songs he learnt in his brewing days in South London and would sit us up on the piano to join in, to Grandmother's manifest distaste. I can only remember

Hokey Pokey, penny a lump
Taste before you buy

But there were many others some of which Grandmother found 'most unsuitable for children'.

"Before dinner everyone assembled in the oak room for a glass of sherry except Aunt Eve and Uncle Sandy who preferred to equip themselves with a couple of mind-numbing 'gin and French' in their room, and we often went in for a talk with them. Sandy was a rather dour Scot who had done well in the City and was now a senior member of Scottish Widows Insurance. Grandmother thoroughly disliked this splinter group drinking separately, and usually took it out on Sandy, because Aunt Eve could give as good as she got. Sandy could not be taken too much to task because he travelled to the City every day and was well in with the Black Market. Some of the items he brought back and gave to Mrs Graham (a fellow Scot) greatly enhanced Grandmother's table.

"Aunt Eve, in her middle forties, was to us unbelievably glamorous with her jet black hair in the style of the 1920s. Beautifully dressed at all times – she never heard of ration coupons – because she had her own dress shop, Ann Blake in South Moulton Street. She got up late and walked about in flowing robes with Turkish cigarettes in a long holder, just about the antithesis in appearance to Grandmother with whom she had a love-hate relationship.

"Reynolds, with his wife and son, had a cottage in the stable-garage yard. He was the son of a Norfolk gamekeeper and had that lovely slow, soft accent of East Anglia. Grandfather eschewed opulent foreign cars and kept Vauxhalls, which he liked because of their solid, decent unflashy Britishness. The largest of his Vauxhalls was laid up on blocks throughout the war, but was polished almost daily. No one ever drove the cars except Reynolds in his uniform. An awkward memory – being taken to the school train at Woking and being put on it with Reynolds carrying my bags, observed by other boys. I persuaded Reynolds never to do this again. Reynolds and Grandfather had a very close relationship and were great friends. Grandmother thought Reynolds was too familiar, but he was indispensable. Reynolds kept the large flock of chickens which produced an endless supply of eggs and birds for the house. He much preferred that sort of work, and felling trees for logs, to driving cars, so the war made his life very much happier. We spent most of our waking hours in the stable yard helping Reynolds and in the company of Grandfather's gun dogs, three black Labradors: Paddy, Johnnie and Frankie. When Paddy, the mother of the other two, became too old to go out shooting, she was allowed to live in the house which was lovely.

"Grandmother was not going to let the war spoil her life which consisted of tennis and bridge, as well bossing the WRVS (Women's Royal Volunteer Service) around for various fundraising events. After breakfast was over she went to the morning room where she was attended by servants for instructions. She also wrote quite a lot of letters and made telephone calls to arrange her social life. I don't think Grandmother intended any unkindness to us but she was incapable of understanding children. I don't know how she coped with her own – not much one supposes. She was totally left behind intellectually by Grandfather's rapid rise to fame and fortune. She wasn't stupid but could make crass remarks. She had no sense of humour and never understood Grandfather's jokes, which she always took quite seriously – 'Oh Frank how could you say such a thing.'

"There were immaculate grass courts as well as a hard court (kept well out of sight) for us to practise on at Red Court. Grandmother for her size and age was amazingly good at tennis. Whatever the weather she wore a fearsomely large sun visor, a sort of Achilles helmet to terrify the opposition. There was never a shortage of people, perfectly clad in white, to play tennis at Red Court. Tea outdoors was the main event of the summer afternoon, replaced by tea indoors to fuel bridge parties during the winter months. Bridge was conducted in total silence except for bidding, and if annoyed by some verbal interference Grandmother would drum the table with her heavily jewelled fingers until silence was restored. She tried to teach us bridge, but it put me off for thirty years. Tea indoors was enlivened by Laura being brought out of her cage by Grandmother and being fed bits of cucumber sandwiches."

It was an illuminating task, typing out these memories in my father's clear handwriting for this book. Most of them touched on a half-remembered story, apart from the depth of his feeling for his mother about which he never spoke. It also slowly became apparent to me that many of the outdoor tasks that he so relished in life came from the time he and his brother spent with either the keeper at Sacombe or Reynolds. They eclipsed the examples set by his own father and uncles, which makes for a curious counterpoise to a story focused on family continuities. We lived with an early nineteenth century oil painting (by a pupil of Turner's) of a ship trying to make safe harbour in a storm that once hung in Red Court. Ida, the old parlour-maid took this off the wall and hid it under her bed when the family pictures were being hurriedly divided up after a death. She was not taking it for herself, but so that my father could have something to remember of his childhood from the oak-panelled room at Red Court.

CHAPTER FIVE

Commander Hugh Rogerson

Every man thinks meanly of himself for not having fought, or not having been at sea.
Samuel Johnson

I greatly admired my grandfather, whom we knew as 'Pop'. He had a merry twinkle to his eye, and we were taught that he had chosen a life of his own, consciously returning to the occupations and landscape of his ancestors, and to the old hands-on crafts of farming and brewing. He had fought in the First World War as a midshipman and sailed the seven seas after this, keeping the Pax Britannica. However, as we got older, we realised that there was a certain ambiguity behind his chosen rural identity, which was evident in his driving fast,

6 July 1914, Jerome versus Rogerson, boxing match at summer sportsday, Royal Naval College, Osborne Palace, Isle of Wight

expensive Italian cars, having all his shirts made by Turner and Asser, his shoes by Lobb and his hats from Bates in Jermyn street. The culture of the well-dressed English gentleman, the perpetual amateur breezing his way through life, was also a strong element. Later, we learned that he had been a determined womaniser, a somewhat swaggering, albeit handsome star of the local hunt and the associated world of point-to-points and steeple chasing. Aunt Marion, who never had a bad word for anyone, did once confide to me in her old age that my grandfather had not been a good husband to Gertie (my grandmother, Gertrude Rochford). Coming from her, this comment spoke volumes. His second marriage, to Olivia Worthington, also ended up very badly, but my father liked to remember them just after the war, an apparently happy couple, riding to hounds together and both delighting in county society. But a schism later tore this chosen life apart. On one hand there was the malting business and the farm, and the hunting and racing that he shared so enthusiastically with his eldest son Barry. On the other was his commitment to his second wife, who aside from any infidelities, was probably angered by his comparative indifference to her only child, his youngest son. I spent many an evening trying to coax my uncle Nico to say one good thing about his father, but the very most he could do was to express some sympathy about what his father had experienced at the Battle of Jutland as a sixteen-year old boy. If we emptied a third bottle, he recalled some hazy memories of some brutal incidents that his father had witnessed during a Chinese civil war, but that seemed to be the outer limit of his affection.

By chance I met an old girlfriend of Nico's in Somerset, who as you will see is a writer. She sent me this letter:

Hawke Term, Dartmouth Royal Naval College

Hugh in command of his first ship, HMS Plucky

Gallows humour, Hugh "strung up"

Hugh with two brother officers, HMS Ganges

Rifle Drill, HMS Ganges

Hugh, Field Master of the Puckeridge & Thurlow Hounds

Meet of the Puckeridge & Thurlow Hounds at Sacombebury, 4 February 1938

Hugh Stanley Rogerson, aged 4 in 1902

"I was twenty years old when I first me the Rogersons; Commander Hugh Rogerson and his second wife Olivia. I was going out with their son Nico and was nervous about meeting his parents. Twenty was young in those days and Nico must have told me something about his father beforehand which made me apprehensive.

"Commander Rogerson was indeed an extremely forceful and charismatic figure, direct, confident and rather overpowering. Although I had lived in Paris for many years, my mother's uncle and first cousins (the Faulkners) were all quite senior in the Royal Navy so I knew roughly what to expect. The difference, as I was to discover later, was his passion for horses and racing, about which I knew nothing, which rather lowered his opinion of me, certainly at first. There was something challenging about him, as if he was testing me, which I experience with Field Marshal Montgomery under similar circumstance several years later. A kind of inspection.

Gone Gay, owned by Lt-Col White and ridden by Lt-Cdr Hugh Rogerson, Enfield Chase Hunt Steeplechase

"His wife could not have been more different. Very beautiful in a slightly unconventional way with wonderful eyes, set far apart, and a soft and rather husky, low voice, just like Nico. I loved her immediately and never felt her judging me although she must have been curious about any girlfriend of her only son's. I can't remember how long Nico and I were together, it was fifty years ago, but when it ended I was saddened, and suspected that she was too. She looked after me once when I was ill and was kindness itself. I really loved her.

"Olivia and Nico were very close, very alike, and when I look back I suspect that Commander Rogerson felt himself outside that closeness, excluded even, and probably resented it. He was often unkind and critical about Nico, unnecessarily. His other sons were much older and Commander Rogerson was quick to dismiss Nico and criticise him as if he was envious of his youngest son's great charm and sweetness, qualities which

he had inherited from his mother and which his father could not understand. It hurt me and surely must have hurt his mother more. And yet, Hugh was a fascinating man. There was something of the bully in him, macho and provocative, such a contrast to his wife who was strong in a completely different way – an inner strength rather than a forceful exterior. He was probably used to a more feisty, reactive woman and I think he may have been frustrated by the bond which he couldn't understand between his wife and her charming son. He never seemed to value Nico's qualities as they were so different from his own. I may have got him wrong but I do have a good memory and the Rogersons made a lasting impression on me."

My grandfather Hugh left behind some papers which Olivia passed on to me. They describe his experience of Jutland and the process of coaling a battleship. There is also an account of being a midshipman written by a childhood colleague in the Navy who became an Admiral and would later become a

Cup Winners and Committee, Newmarket & Thurlow Point to Point, 1934

Hugh on his much beloved Sarah Jane, *bought unbroken for £20 and a round of drinks at Barnet Horse Fair*

Marriage of Getrude Rochford to Hugh Rogerson, Brompton Oratory, 1925

Suffolk neighbour. They were in the same term and served in the same ship. The same typewriter was used for all three narratives, and they complement each other. I find them fascinating, but I am both a historian and his grandson. They also lead us too far from our theme, so I have been placed them right at the end of this book, Appendix Four.

Hugh had attended the Royal Navy's prep school at Osborne (which took over Queen Victoria's seaside palace in the Isle of Wight) before he went onto Dartmouth Royal Naval College, Hawke Term. His youthful baptism of fire had been one of the initiatives of Churchill, who when serving as First Lord of the Admiralty was keen to get young officers more fully at home with life at sea. Hugh served as a midshipman in the great battleship HMS *Indomitable* from September 1915 and experienced the Battle of Jutland. This would later be followed by a torpedo course at HMS *Victory*. Then right at the end of the war he had his own tiny command, the minesweeper HMS Plucky part of the Fourteenth Flotilla working out of Inverness. After that he was transferred to the China Station, sailing out on HMS *Colombo* and

then patrolling the Yangtze in the gunboat HMS *Cricket*. He left the Navy in 1922 (staying on the Reserve List) and got married in July 1925 in the Brompton Oratory. His father, Frank Rogerson, was able to set him up, by buying one of the maltings businesses in Ware, John Harrington, which he would later amalgamate with the one owned by the Page-Croft family. His first wife, Gertrude Rochford, was the daughter of Thomas Rochford who was the third generation of his family to run a nursery business. Exotic plants were grown under hundreds of acres of greenhouses at Turnford Hall, Hertfordshire. Throughout the Second World War he was stationed at HMS *Ganges*, a Naval training school. His commanding officer wrote: 'A first rate Divisional Officer with an outstanding knowledge of men. A natural leader with strong personality, a keen sense of humour and essentially loyal. An excellent mixer and an excellent mess-mate.'

CHAPTER SIX

Two English Gentlemen:
John Rogerson and Michael Rogerson

A gentleman is one who puts more into the world than he takes out.
Julie Andrews

My parents both adored John Rogerson who they treated as the head of the family. John Rogerson owned and bred race-horses, served as a steward of the Jockey Club and was High Sherriff of Sussex in 1961. He and his wife Eileen lived at Guildenhurst, a sprawling, much improved-upon and extended farmhouse full of oak beams and ancient wooden floors. It was the centre of their estate in Sussex – complete with its own garage, pub and farms, topped up by a shoot in Suffolk conveniently near their racing stables at Newmarket. Their life was dominated by the racing and the shooting season, backed up by hunting and fishing. Uncle John was also an exceptionally good all-round sportsmen, who could do anything but yet never let go of the easy smile of the amateur. It was the playing, not the winning that counted. As a young man he took the greatest delight in tennis and skiing.

John served throughout the Second World War as a squadron leader on the staff of Air Chief Marshall Sir William Sholto Douglas. He was part of the team that plotted the first Anglo-American invasion (Operation Torch) better known as the Casablanca landings as well as 'The Man Who Never Was' – an attempt to distract the Germans from the next amphibious operation which was the invasion of Sicily. My father never contradicted this tale but hinted that later on in the war his uncle had an additional, and even more delicate task, which was to chronicle the intimate habits of some of our allies. To this end he was seconded as a dashing, well-connected aide-de-camp to various American Air Marshalls to help settle them into English society. Sholto Douglas, as well as being one of the hero commanders of the Battle of Britain and an architect of the Normandy

Landings, had also been very keen on an invasion of Rhodes and the Dodecanese (which was opposed by the USA) so there may be a whiff of truth to these slivers of family gossip. John never spoke about his experiences in the war but by chance the children of one of his wartime colleagues (called Moffat who married very late in life) were at Cottesmore and had got their old father to talk.

After the war John suffered with cancer of the throat, but the surgeons saved him. They were forced to cut out his voice box, but he managed to teach himself to speak again, though only in brief half-sentences, which were effectively created by a sort of whispered belch. He had a gold rivet in his throat which he covered up with a cravat when not wearing a tie. He modestly claimed that it was only this that gave him the reputation of being a wit, for as he was forced to ration his words to a brief half-sentence, he tightened his language up and made the most of it. His preparatory struggle for breathe with which to speak also helped to silence his audience, so there was something almost theatrical about the final delivery, which my father (who adored his uncle) compared to Patrick Campbell's famous manipulation of his stutter on television. He was also a fabulous tipper, and my father enjoyed watching how his uncle's generosity, got them immediate attention from hall porters and the best tables from the maître d'. This is also how Dinah Rogerson, my aunt by marriage to Uncle Nico remembers first meeting the Rogerson family.

"My Uncle Tim was born in 1931. He was ten years younger than my father, Malise Nicolson. He married Valda Rogerson. Their wedding was at St Peters Eaton Square and the reception was at the

John Rogerson, skiing above Murren with the west face of the Eiger in the background

Squadron-Leader John Rogerson served on the staff of Air Chief Marshall Sholto Douglas

Hyde Park Hotel. Denis Mountain was best man. My sister (Emma Nicolson) was a bridesmaid and the wedding photographs show her standing next to Matthew Rogerson who is wearing a smart kilt in the Nicolson tartan. I was ten and considered too old to be a bridesmaid. Who would have thought that fifty years on I would be married to Nico, Valda's first cousin Nico.

"I left school (St Marys Wantage) in July 1963 with rather a paltry selection of O levels. That September I moved to London to do a course called 'Look and Learn' which my parents, who weren't remotely interested in the arts, felt (surprisingly) would enrich my education. Our days were spent visiting London museums, art galleries, exhibitions and the like. The seeds were definitely sown during those few months for an appreciation of art and antiques which led me to my career in Interior Design. My parents lived in Cheshire which was considered a bit far to travel, so most weekends I went to stay at Streele Farm, the home of my Uncle Tim and Aunt Valda and their two boys, my first cousins, Alastair and Euan.

"The highlight of these weekends was Sunday lunch with John and Eileen Rogerson, Valda's parents, who lived nearby at Guildenhurst Manor. I became very fond of John and Eileen who shared my passion for jigsaw puzzles. John Rogerson's generosity was legendary. My rather meagre allowance was hugely benefited by a shilling per jigsaw piece that I managed to fill in."

To this day, there is an annual race held at Fontwell Park in November, set up as a Memorial to John Rogerson. John was born 31 July 1902 and was sent to Felsted School in Essex where he proved himself an all-round sportsman with a particular gift for tennis, which continued through his years at Cambridge. He worked in the Stock Exchange but his life was transformed by falling in love with Eileen, 'a most natural, unspoilt sweet person'.

In contrast, Eileen's father was the Midas of his generation, a towering figure of international finance whose gold-plated Rolls Royce would be escorted by police motorcyclists as if he were a Prince, from his house in Mayfair to his office in the City of London. Sir Solomon Joel had survived

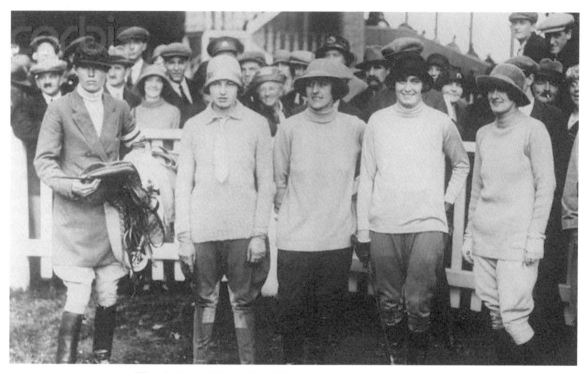

Eileen Joel (second from right) 1925 winner of the Newmarket Town Plate

a number of assassination attempts, kept a string of mistresses, collected Morland pictures, owned theatres, a steam yacht, mines and railways and gave famously lavish parties before the principal Race Meetings. His guests would be near drowned in vintage champagne, but Sir Solomon only ever sipped at a single glass, never letting down his guard.

Solomon was one of the three sons of Joel Joel who ran the King of Prussia pub in London's Jewish East End. Joel's brother-in-law was Barney Isaacs better known as Barney Barnato (1851-1897). Barney was an East-End wide boy, who used his wits to survive, dealing in old clothes and discarded theatre tickets while still a child. As a youth he could hold his own as a prize-fighting boxer but also doubled up as a support singer for his brother Harry in the East End music halls. After a spot of trouble, Barney took a 'steerage ticket' out to South Africa but by the time he had arrived, the Kimberley Diamond rush was over. However he stayed on, getting to know the land and its characters, while the miners loved talking with a man who could both sing, joke and fight with his fists. Barney put his street-trading

John at a race meeting

Eileen's father, Sir Solomon Joel

skills to work and started to learn about the pricing of diamonds. At this time, the Kimberley pit was divided into an ants' nest of small claims (each with their own boundary walls made accessible by a web of steel cables linked to the high ground) which made for a Babel-like vision of activity, highly unstable excavations and an erratic market-place. The miners grew to trust Barney, who paid cash upfront which he combined with an open-handed generosity with cigars and bottles of champagne at the bar. Barney ploughed his profits back into the business. His first venture was to buy four worked-out claims, which he made good under efficient new management, for he had also been chatting up some innovative young mining engineers. So he asked for his three young nephews (Solomon, Jack and Wolf Joel) to come out from London to help him, for you needed your back covered in those days. There were shoot-outs, foreign agents, discrete financial backers and any number of secret deals, one of which culminated in the Jameson Raid (and a spate of treason trials) while another led to the emergence of the Diamond Syndicate. A fierce rivalry grew between Cecil Rhodes and Barney Barnato for control of Kimberley pit which pushed

Guildenhurst Manor, Sussex

up prices until they decided to bury the hatchet and create De Beers with the world's largest known cheque. This would be followed by some internal infighting. Wolf Joel was killed in a shoot-out in the head office and Barney Barnato drowned off Madeira, falling off the back of a liner whilst smoking a cigar at midnight in the company of a nephew. Solomon Joel ended up as the new boss, but with a whiff of sulphur about him, like an Anglo-Jewish Gatsby or a London-dwelling Russian oligarch. Sir Solomon became a most determined owner and breeder of racehorses and bought Sir Edmund Cassels racing stables outside Newmarket in 1922. This would have many satisfying associations. Cassels had been one of the most socially prominent bankers of the turn-of-the-century, and as a personal friend of King Edward VII had been a role model for British Jews. Sir Solomon had married Nellie, a beautiful actresss (Ellen Ridley) with whom he had five children.

Sir Solomon was possessive of his daughters and would disinherit his daughter Doris for marrying outside the faith. His son Wolf was killed in action in the First World War and Dudley drowned whilst saving someone's life at sea. Apart from her brother Stanhope, Eileen was the sole survivor. She shared her father's passion for horses and had proved herself a really accomplished rider. In 1925 she entered the Newmarket Town Plate, against an open field of men and women. This four-mile race for amateurs had been established by King Charles II in the seventeenth century. The King had won it in 1671 and it remains the oldest race in the world to retain its original rules. In 1925 Eileen Joel won the race on Hogier, the first woman so to do. She became the apple of her father's eye. She was also wise enough not to spark off a row with her autocratic old father and persuaded her boyfriend John Rogerson to wait until Sir Solomon was dead.

Eileen Joel and John Rogerson got married in 1931. Thirty years later, their daughter Valda Rogerson would win the Newmarket Town Plate on Vulpes, and twenty-threes after that their grand-daughter Alex Embericos won it on Summons in 1984. It is a unique three-generational female achievement, which any Rogerson can delight in, while saluting the fact that two other Joel women (Solna in 1948 and Diana Thompson-Jones in 1964) have also taken the Newmarket Town Plate, which probably shows

Eileen's horse, Athens Wood *ridden by Lester Piggot won the St Leger in 1971*

us where the talent comes from. Valda first married Tim Nicolson and brought up two boys (Euan and Alastair) at the isolated sanctuary of Steele Farm on the edge of the Guildenhurst estate. Valda had a daughter Alex with her second husband, the dashingly good-looking Nick Embiricos who had grown up in the Bahamas. The Embiricos family are now scattered all over the world, but originally came from Andros in Greece where they established one of the worlds great shipping lines. Nick and Valda bred racehorses at Barkfold Manor (their home in Sussex) as well as placing their horses with such famous trainers as Josh Gifford. In 1981, their horse Aldaniti won the Grand National which gave an unexpected zest to their lives. A film was made about how Bob Champion (the jockey who rode Aldaniti to victory) had survived cancer of the bollocks, and not only survived but had gone on to triumph at the Grand National. The success of the film inspired them to set up the Bob Champion trust which raises money for research into testicular cancer.

Valda, John and Eileen's daughter with her grandfather Frank at RedCourt

Valda Rogerson in command of the governess cart

Valda Rogerson winning the Newmarket Town Plate

Wedding of Valda Rogerson and Tim Nicolson, youngest son of Sir Kenneth and Lady Nicolson was held at St Peter's Eaton Square. Sir Denis Mountain was the bestman, pageboys Mathew Rogerson, Christopher and Diana Thomson-Jones and Andrew and Joanna Brudenell-Bruce

MR. T. J. S. NICOLSON AND MISS V. S. D. ROGERSON

The marriage took place yesterday at St. Peter's, Eaton Square, of Mr. Timothy John Shuttleworth Nicolson, youngest son of Sir Kenneth and Lady Nicolson, of Norton Bavant Manor, Warminster, Wiltshire, and Miss Valda Solna Deirdre Rogerson, only daughter of Mr. and Mrs. John Rogerson, of Guildenhurst Manor, Billingshurst, Sussex. The Rev. H. L. Johnston and the Rev. W. A. Simmonds took part in the service.

The bride, who was given away by her father, wore a gown of heavy white satin with a fitting bodice, high neckline, long sleeves, and a full skirt falling into a train. Her tulle veil was held in place by a diamond tiara and she carried a bouquet of Eucharis lilies, lilies-of-the-valley, stephanotis, and freesia. Three pages and three child bridesmaids attended her. The pages, Matthew Rogerson, Christopher Thomson Jones, and Andrew Brudenell-Bruce, wore the Nicolson tartan, with white silk blouses and white sealskin sporrans. The bridesmaids, Emma Nicolson, Diana Thomson Jones, and Joanna Brudenell-Bruce, wore full-skirted white tulle dresses with narrow white satin sashes. Their head-dresses were of scarlet polyanthus roses, and they carried posies to match. Mr. Denis Mountain was best man.

A reception was held at the Hyde Park Hotel, and the honeymoon is being spent abroad.

Press clipping, "Mr T.J.S.Nicolson and Miss V.S.D.Rogerson"

Alex Embiricos, like her mother, and like her grandmother, won the Newmarket Town Plate

The annual John Rogerson Cup at Fontwell Races

There was a seven-year gap between Frank Rogerson's first three children (Eve, Hugh and John) and the two youngest children, Michael and Betty. By this time in his life, Frank had more time to spend with his children and was a wealthy man. Michael Rogerson wrote his own memoir, *In and Out of School* (printed in 1989). Like all self-published books (this one included) it rambles, but I found it touchingly revealing of the friendship between Michael and his father Frank. Michael kept all his father's letters, and they reveal a cheerful, easy relationship. They were also confident enough with each other, to cross the line and now and then tell some home truths. As an old man himself, Michael could look back and write, 'I think we enjoyed real companionship. In school holidays my fondest memory was meeting him off the train on his daily return from work, and after a slice of cake and a whisky and soda, we would do something together.' This habit continued, with golfing and fishing expeditions undertaken throughout Frank's life, as well as exploring Norway, the Alps and southern France together . Frank would begin his letters, 'My Dear old boy', or 'My Dear Mike' and often conclude with some popular verse. One cherished letter quoted an American gospel song written by Austin Miles (1868-1956) which would be read at Michael's own funeral.

Little more kindness and a little less creed,
A little more giving and a little less greed;
A little more smile and a little less frown,
A little less kicking a man when he's down;
A little more "we" and a little less "I,"
A little more laugh and a little less cry;
A few more flowers on the pathway of life,
And fewer on graves at the end of the strife

Michael confessed that 'I was spoilt. Life was too easy and I was protected.' Aged nine he went to Uplands House prep school, followed by Marlborough, then up to Sydney Sussex College at Cambridge, then a year in France where he fell in love with a beautiful Norwegian, Eva Knap. On his twenty first birthday he was given money to buy a car and presented with a gold watch inscribed 'Whom the Gods love die young. May you always be such.' This wish came true, for Michael kept hold of a sort of childlike wonder all his life. In his turn,

he was an outstandingly good father, and this warm and easy relationship would be passed on by all his three children, Mark, Matthew and Mary-Lou, to their own children. In conversation with my second cousins, Thomas Rogerson and John Rogerson, I have observed with interest how this tradition of easy companionship between the generations has continued down the line.

Michael learned about teaching by working for two years (1933-35) at his old school Uplands House which had moved from its original home in Epsom to Buchan House. In 1936 he showed the glint of his ambition, and broke away from Upland House (taking seventeen boys with him) and brought a stake in Cottesmore school which was then based in Hove and run by an elderly headmaster called Forster. In 1939 he married Marion Brownrigg who he had first met when he had taught at Fernden (working for her father) for a term. They went to Capri for their honeymoon but returned in time to move Cottesmore to Wales during the war. Michael was called up to join the army in 1941 and served as a Captain in the Transport Corps. He was not

Michael with his father Frank having challenged the two head waiters at Gleneagles to a round of Golf

Mr and Mrs John Rogerson

Aldaniti, winner of the Grand National, ridden by Bob Champion and owned by Mr and Mrs Nicolas Embiricos

Michael with his first car, a gift from his father

Michael with an even better model

Michael Rogerson, third headmaster of Cottesmore in succession to Geoffrey Davison-Brown and Harry Strong-Forster

a military man but retained happy memories of the Welsh platoon under his command as well as witnessing the devastation of France after the D-Day landings at first hand. Mark and Mary-Lou were born during these war years. After Forster died Michael was permitted to leave the army in order to run the school. In 1946 Michael bought Buchan Hill house and farm, sold up the old school buildings in Hove (to a Roman Catholic school) and moved Cottesmore to its palatial grounds. The following year his bank of energy and enthusiasm was tested to the full when Marion caught polio and spent a year in hospital. To celebrate her recovery they had one more child, Mathew.

I knew Michael Rogerson well. The first round of our relationship was not good. It was almost as if the rivalry between him and his older brother Hugh had continued unto the third generation. I was not good at any ball games or spoken languages, which were the two things in which my great-uncle excelled. He was also finally feeling too old for the 24/7 round-the-clock job of being a hands-on headmaster. Fortunately while I was at Cottesmore his son Mark formally took over (in 1973) and

Mark Rogerson was born 29 April 1942 in St Brenda's nursing home, Clifton while his father was in an army boot camp alongside 150 Welsh miners

Mary-Lou Rogerson was born 1 August 1945, just after Peace had been won

Michael had the good sense to take himself off for a whole year, on a round-the-world tour. The contrast was astonishing to behold, most especially in the qualities of the French lessons. Instead of having my head boxed by a chalk duster as my great uncle tried to teach me how to tell the time in French (which I foolishly did not yet know in English), we sang French songs to accompany Mark Rogerson on his guitar.

As a seventeen-year old, I started on a completely different relationship with my great-uncle Michael. My parents then lived in Gibraltar and flights departed from Gatwick, so during my gap-year travels I often found myself staying at Cottesmore. Michael was kind enough to guess that I could do with some paid work. He was involved in the second great project of his life, of turning the estate farm into a golf course with a courtyard clubhouse alongside his son Mathew. He was an effervescent boss, happy to try things out, to learn from experience, to let you have a go. He was also exuberantly proud of his vegetable garden and his chicken run. Eggs at breakfast were brought to the boil in a silver spirit lamp. He also kept a genuinely hospitable door open to the world. One afternoon we skipped off work (mending a tree house which he had built for golfers to tee off from) and went off to cheer up his elder sister, who had been moved into an old people's home to be nearer to her younger sister and two brothers. Aunt Eve was allowed to bring her own furniture (and drinks cabinet) so we left having had one too many Gin and Dubonnets. On the way home, Michael was stopped by the police, and was potentially in trouble, not only for being over the limit but for being behind the wheel of a favourite old car (a battered old citroen) that was normally confined within the drives of the Cottesmore estate. It did not have an MOT, or insurance or any legal existence but it did have an old golf bag in the back of the car. The golf bag allowed Michael to open up a conversation with the young policeman, and then having discovered a shared sporting passion he confessed his desire to have some of 'the force' on board as founding members of his new golf club. We returned home safely. It was an impressive demonstration of calm, good manners and the gentle art of negotiation. He might have been given a lot by his own father, but he wasted not a penny of his inheritance. He also tried to fair to all three of his children. Mark had been given the school, Mathew was given the golf course, so he gave his daughter Mary-Lou his name on Lloyds in the Gardner-Mountain syndicate. In the 1960's a name on Lloyds Insurance was a licence to make money, and so in financial terms Mary-Lou had been given the richest inheritance. There were only fifteen hundred such 'names' in the whole of Britain marshalled between seventy syndicates. Michael was not to know that this generous gift was about to become toxic, for a name had unlimited liability. In the late 1970's, the gilded profitability of Lloyds went into reverse and various syndicates were bled dry. Michael felt guilty about this, not that you ever heard so much as a flicker of complaint from his daughter. He tried to make some amends, including leaving Mary-Lou the house that he and Marion had built in the heart of the Cottesmore estate. Typically Mary-Lou mentions none of this, but did kindly send me a letter describing "the Miss Rogerson" period of her life.

Cottesmore was my much-loved home, but as a middle child between Mark and Matthew I had a happy but slightly unusual childhood. It was a wonderful playground for a child but with my two brothers away at my Uncle's prep school, Fernden in Haslemere, I was very often lonely. The nursery with Nanty our much loved Nanny, was a happy place, a cosy nest but I had very few visitors to play with. We saw little of our parents during term time at the school, but holidays together have special memories for us when Dad and Mum let their hair down. At boarding school at Southover Manor in Lewes I found my love of art though I was desperately homesick (or maybe I should I say 'dogsick') as I loved those dogs. My parents obviously thought I needed some of my rough edges smoothed down after that, golly they must have been pretty rough edges as I was first bundled off to Mont Fertile finishing school in Switzerland, then various courses for young ladies in London followed by dress making at Katinka, modelling or rather a 'charm course' at Lucy Clayton (where I found my neck was too short to be a successful model),

Mary-Lou with Nanty (Mrs Edith Challis) who came back to help the Rogerson family when Marion went down with polio in 1947

Wedding of Mary-Lou Rogerson with Francis Hussey

guitar lessons, singing lessons, 'Look and Learn' course, secretarial and art courses and then apparently I was ladylike enough to be a debutante and 'Come Out' for the London season in 1963. I found it all agony and it just wasn't ME, but in those days I had no choice, and now I wish I had appreciated more all the refinements that my parents thought would turn me into an accomplished and confident person. Tra-la!

I eventually found myself working in a glamorous fashion shop in Knightsbridge, the 'heart of smart ' in London where notably, I foiled a theft of priceless silk dresses and had to help a Chinese customer try on a ball gown …. a Chinese man that is. I was shocked but managed to keep my cool, at just 19 years old I was very innocent! Mary Quant, Biba, mini-skirts, hot pants, buckets of makeup and The Beatles music were all the rage in the mid 1960's. Inspired by this experience and with a small legacy from my Grandmother Rogerson, I opened 'Sheba' my clothes 'Boutique' and fashion

Wedding of Mathew Rogerson and Susan Cheeseman

mecca in Cuckfield, a charming and wealthy little village in Sussex. A Georgian town house semi above the high street it was big enough for me to turn the upper floors and basement into accommodation to let. What had I let myself in for ! My first tenant turned out to be a prostitute, then came an alcoholic 78 year old, a divorced milkman asked me up to his room to take photos of me ….in the nude, an Indian couple who wafted curry everywhere and did a moonlight flit owing me two months rent! Could I have chosen worse tenants for my first business venture?

I studied carefully which fashion houses to choose to stock up 'Sheba'. I had absolutely no idea what I was doing but The fashion shows I turned up to were a dream and after being plied with a strong G and T or glass of wine I ploughed in and spent money, mostly that I didn't have, with gusto. Over the years it became a must go destination for all the fashionable young in Sussex, and then on the 4th April 1970 I got

Matthew Rogerson playing golf with his father for a press shoot. Together they would create the Cottesmore Golf Course, slowly convert the farm buildings and build Buchan House and Challis Wood between 1971–73

married to Francis Hussey and our glorious wedding was celebrated at my wonderful home for the first 24 years of my life, Cottesmore School and Buchan Hill House.

At the end of his life, Michael Rogerson became a bit of a handful, trotting around at high speed with a mane of white hair flowing in the breeze, a bit like a Sussex version of King Lear, now and then muttering under his breath, 'stupid little arse, stupid little arse.' But he had sewn affection all around him.

The day he died I had a most particular dream. His children (Mark, Matthew and Mary-Lou and their partners and their many children) were mourning beside the frame of his old body, laid out like a waxwork on his bed. But his youthful spirit, without so much as backward glance had passed through a gauze curtain that shimmered with light. He was running off into the next

adventure without so much as a parting glance at his family. He had written a letter to his children on 18 November 1989, asking them not to keep him alive in a hospital once he became a senile old man. He also wrote:

I have had a most wonderful time on earth and only hope I have contributed a little to the advancement of goodness – I have no views about the after life – though I wish I had. I think the only things that matters is what one does when alive. I am sorry I didn't do more because I had so many opportunities. Love to you all and may God's spirit help you.

The family of Michael and Marion Rogerson, exploding with grandchildren over a bench in the garden of Cottesmore **Back row:** *Annabelle (holding dog), Francis, Mathew holding Helen, Michael and Mary Lou.* **Front row:** *Sacha, Tom on the lap of his mother Cathryn, Mark (then, the second Rogerson headmaster of Cottesmore), Sophie, Marion, Lucy, Susan, Sam*

Buchan Farm has a French feel to it and may have been built by French prisoners of war. By 1823 it was part of an estate of 3,000 acres assembled by Thomas Broadwood from the profits of his piano manufactory, then passed into the hands of the lawyer Thomas Erskine (who rose to become Lord Chancellor) before later passing into the possession of Philip Saillard who built New Buchan House in 1883, throwing £40,000 into the project

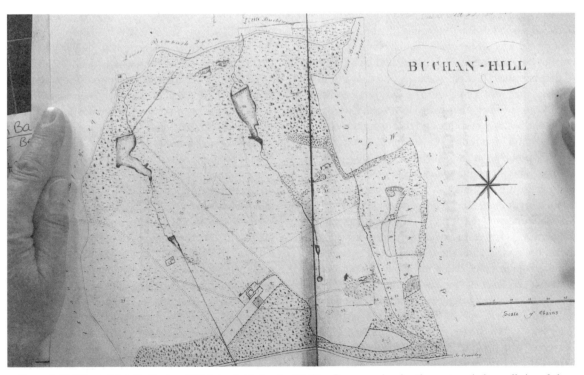

Copy of Old Estate Map for Buchan Hill being held open by Mathew Rogerson, showing the comparatively small size of the original Buchan House, but the large farm-house courtyard as well as the walled garden. The land was 'marginal at best' and largely used for coppiced woodlands, cropped by fence makers and charcoal burners.

Cottesmore Golf and Country Club was up and running by 1976, after which Mathew had sufficient income for its continual development

Betty Rogerson was the youngest of this brood of five strong characters. She could be self-effacing 'I was born to be a play-mate for Michael' and lacked some of the charisma of her older siblings. She did not think much of her own looks, and her face was certainly more equine rather than pretty as a young woman, but as she became a mother and then a grandmother, she grew into her strong looks. I think in the end, her life was probably more contended than any of her siblings. She was bright, observant, no one's fool and had dignity. I can remember standing next to her at a family wedding as the groom (or perhaps it was the bestman) pour too much praise on John Rogerson as the perfect godfather. I watched Betty's eyebrow grow ever more arched, until she whispered (quite audibly) 'Rubbish! John never did a thing but has obviously written a very large cheque this morning.'

Betty married a bright, handsome but essentially self-sufficient cricketeer, Patrick Ward Milligan (educated at Winchester) just before the war. Uncle Pat served with the Queens Royal Regiment in France as part of the BEF, then was posted to Iraq and fought in the Western Desert, ending up a staff officer with the rank of Lt-Colonel. They had a daughter Jennifer who was born in RedCourt during the war, followed by a son, Richard Milligan. Uncle Pat rose to become the senior partner at Sedgwick Collis and then Chairman of Lloyds Insurance. Jennifer married a dashing young man from South Africa, Richard Wills who did well at Lloyds. Their son Simon Wills was another cousin sent to Cottesmore and went onto Charterhouse together, where we would companionably walk to take a lavish tea at the Old Coach House, Eashing off Mrs Patrick Milligan, his grandmother, my great aunt. Aunt Betty would stock up her drinks cabinet, so that we could smuggle small (but very popular) cans of beer back to school. Years later I found Simon running a wine bar in Fulham. He would tell me stories about walking across Sudan while at the same time explaining to me the dozen tricks with which one's staff could intelligently plunder the turnover. He had already had a go at selling vintage cars, and would set up all sorts of businesses, for he had an infectious charm and an easy way with customers. When last heard of, he was setting up a dry-cleaning business and a new life for himself in Majorca. His younger brother Patrick is a financial advisor (alongside his girlfriend Sarah Chevenix Trench) for a 'single client', a sufficiently profitable enterprise for them to own His and Hers helicopters.

Rogerson family arranged around their young cousin Allenby, smiling in his school uniform. From left, Hugh with hands in his pockets, his mother Florence in hat, cousin Gladys Rogerson (daughter of Uncle Charlie), Frank in centre of doorway, Betty Rogerson beside him, Miriam Rogerson, Gertie (wife of Hugh Rogerson), Patrick Milligan with dalmatian.

Betty Rogerson skiing with her sister-in-law Eileen and brother John Rogerson in Switzerland before the war

Marriage of Jennifer Milligan to Richard Wills

Betty Rogerson or the arm of her father, Frank Rogerson, Witley Church, 1934.

Mr and Mrs Patrick Milligan outside their first home, Shamley Green

CHAPTER SEVEN

Man of Talent:
Frank Rogerson (1872–1946)

He who trades good copper for fake silver swindles his ancestors.
Japanese proverb

Frank Rogerson was born in Hoddesdon on 14 April, 1872, the seventh child of Lucy and Josiah Rogerson. Frank proved himself clever and inventive, industrious and successful. He was fascinated by science and had a classless ease about him which he combined with a genuine delight in his family and in life. This was not just about the ownership of his children but included all the families of his seven siblings. Frank could sketch and draw, he loved the silent concentration of fishing, the easy chatter of the golf course, the companionship of shooting and the

buzz of the race-course. He could also occupy the centre of the stage, recite verse from memory, compose speeches and could sit at a piano and sing the drinking songs of the pubs of South London – many of them shockingly indecent. Right at the end of his life, during the Second World War, his house became a safe haven lived in by three generations of his family, removed from the anxiety of rationing by a well-stocked cellar, chicken runs and a huge vegetable garden. As we have already heard, my father was one of these refugee-Rogersons put up a Red Court. His cousin Jennifer was

This page and overleaf: sketches by Frank, pen and ink copies. Above: Cow and Calf, made when he was fifteen.

Georgina

Three terriers

Man of Talent: Frank Rogerson (1872–1946)

born there, whilst her father fought in North Africa and there are also photographs of Nico Rogerson in his pram, whose own father was back in his naval uniform. Frank (even as an old man) had not lost any of his interest in life and had become so fascinated by the process of digestion that he had acquired a stomach pump. Tomato skins were then analysed for their resistance to acids. He also made his own tonic water but his experiments to preserve cooked chickens were not so successful and ended up in explosions. According to my father, his grandmother (Florence Allenby) was not so liberal and would get herself consumed in petty social anxieties, such as where to receive the under-butler who had been promoted to a captain during the war and wanted to come back and pay them a friendly visit. My father remembered her more idiotic sayings, such as 'the advertisements speak very highly of it.' But she clearly had her own style. She liked to be cajoled into joining a game of tennis (urged on by some fresh young guest of her children) before revealing a devastatingly strong forehand drive.

Florence was born in 1876 and died on 20 November 1963. My sister remembered visiting her once, a vast helpless old woman in white, being brought her meals on trays. My elder brother also recalls 'an enormous woman lying motionless on her death bed, and I kissed her right hand.'

Her family originated from Cumberland, where there are lots of name-related Allonby, Ellonbi, Aleynebey, Alemby, Alanbye found marked on old maps, for 'Alein' is spur and 'By' translates as farm. Florence's grandfather was called Joseph Stamper Allenby. He was born in 1799 at Crosscanonby, Allenby Bay close to Roman Milefort 21, on the western edge of Hadrian's wall. He became a doctor and established a practised in Warwick. Florence's father was Lewis Charles Allenby, who was born in Warwick in 1847. He moved down to London as a young man, working in a Bank before setting up his own business, as a linen merchant. In 1891 he was living at 17 Rosendale Road, Dulwich. Florence's eldest brother (who might have been called Hedsworth) died of tubercolosis, but her two younger brothers Charles Williamson and Clarence Edward survived. One of her nephews, Kenneth Allenby, became a doctor like his great-grandfather, and sent his sons Charles and Edward to be educated alongside their Rogerson cousins at Cottesmore.

Frank grew up in Myddelton House which stood directly opposite the Brewery at Hoddesdon on the other side of the High Street

Frank Rogerson was born and brought up in Myddleton House in the heart of Hoddesdon. It was a busy household with nine children and half a dozen servants. Frank was sent off to Cranbrook, a boarding school set in the healthy air of the Sussex coast outside Eastbourne, where he played football in the first eleven. Harry, the youngest of all the Rogerson brothers, joined him two years later. School uniforms were handed down through a long line of brothers, and the inherited football boots had long lost any flexibility in their leathers. Frank used to joke that it was the hand-me-down boots that inspired him to make his own money. In 1891 (aged nineteen) he was in a training position at a brewery in Wallingford. Four years later, aged just twenty-three he was taken on as the manager of the Stockwell Brewery in Stockwell Green, South London by its owner Charles Hammerton. Frank, like all his brothers, would have been intimate with the secret processes of brewing from infancy, by just growing up in his father's household and watching his careful management of the great works at Hoddesdon. But he, like all but one of his brothers had been carefully placed by their father as apprentices elsewhere. Frank himself invented a number of processes that improved the craft of brewing. The one that we know about was patented in the USA (serial number 387,141 dated 22 November 1910). It purified air in order to control the brewing yeast so that it would not become contaminated. From the tone of the Articles of Agreement with the Stockwell Brewery (not officially signed and sealed until 17 April 1896,) Frank was already standing on his own merits. In this agreement, the proprietor, Charles Hammerton appears to have given him complete control of the business. Frank pledged his 'whole services, attention and energies to the same in brewing, managing, conducting, superintending and improving..to the utmost of his power and ability.' In return he was to be given £450 a year, in four quarterly payments, but crucially he was also to be allowed a share in all increased business, initially fixed at three pence for every extra barrel sold. It was a good salary, probably equivalent to about £60,000 a year in today's money. Some further insight into his new position is given by a letter from his father.

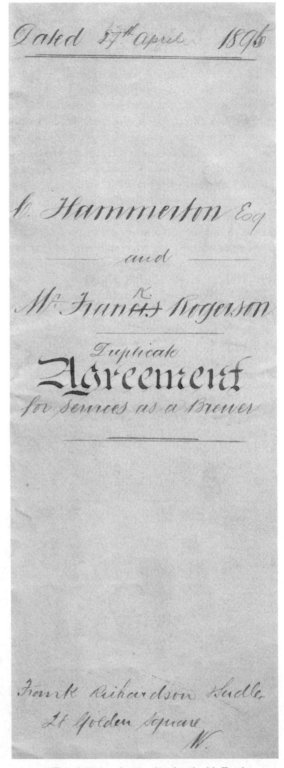

"Francis" crossed out and replaced with Frank

Articles of Agreem

Seventeenth day of April
eight hundred and ninety five Bet
Hammerton of the Stockwell
in the County of Surrey Common Bre
and Frank Rogerson of 2
Stockwell aforesaid Brewer of the o

1. **Witness** that for the consideration hereinafter
said Francis Rogerson doth hereby agree with the sai
that he the said Francis Rogerson shall and will i
during the term of One year to be computed from
of March One thousand eight hundred and ninet
from year to year at the will of the parties the on
three calendar months notice in writing of his inte
this Agreement become be and continue the Brewer
Charles Hammerton in his trade or business of a Com
Stockwell Brewery aforesaid and shall and will du
give up his whole time services attention and energ
in Brewing managing conducting superintendin
the same to the utmost of his power and ability

2. **And** also shall and will during the said ter
all such acts matters or things in about or relatin
or business as he the said Charles Hammerton shal
direct order or appoint.

3. **And** shall not nor will at any time hereafter

Original articles of Agreement between Charles Hammerton, owner of Stockwell brewery to engage
Frank Rogerson as manager (aged just twenty-three) in 1895

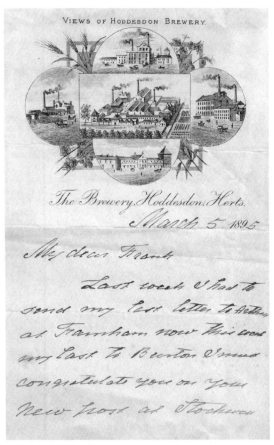

Letter dated 5 March 1895 from Josiah Rogerson to "My dear Frank" with views of the Hoddesdon brewery complex

The Brewery, Hoddesdon, Hertfordshire.
5 March 1895

My dear Frank,

Last week I had to send my last letter to Arthur [his eldest brother] at Farnham now this week my last to Burton [to one of Frank's other brothers working at the brewing centre of Burton on Trent]. I must congratulate you on your new post at Stockwell and trust you will be happy and comfortable but I am afraid you will have all your work cut out to put things right but you will do it. It [the annual salary] ought to have been £500 – but that will come allright no doubt. I trust these few lines will find you well we have all had bad colds and cannot get out of them. I shall be pleased to see this weather go – I should not go in for flats you will be one if you do – get some nice rooms. I should not get far away from the Brewery or Maltings, the nearer you are the better. I shall be very pleased to see you home again for a few days. I am very pleased that Manners [probably Frank's previous employer] is behaving so nicely though I daresay that he is very sorry to lose you – I am sorry to hear of poor James – it is too bad of the lad to treat him so. How do you find trade? We are very quiet in Beer but very busy in Spirits. I shall be very glad when this cold weather goes as I am very sick of it now.

My dear boy I am very tired so will close with our united fond love God bless you –

I am your ever-loving Father
J. W. S. Rogerson.

It seems that Hammerton's Brewery was at a bit of a low ebb in 1895 but Frank seems to have deliberately taken a salary below what his father thought right in order to take a share in any future profits. There was to be no worry about becoming 'flat broke'. Within a few years Frank had transformed the rundown old brewery, and as well as supplying traditional outlets such as the pubs he launched an aggressive advertising campaign for his new range of bottled beers. One famous poster campaign urged mothers to drink Hammerton's Oatmeal Stout if they wanted healthy babies and a plentiful supply of milk. According to his eldest son Frank also employed rougher methods. He arranged for teams of hearty drinkers to tour the south London pubs, who would loudly demand Hammerton's beer and would indignantly refuse to drink anything else. Their visits guaranteed great initial business for any publican who decided to stock Frank's beer aware that a prolonged refusal could cause these same drinkers to return and grow ever more violent and disruptive in their demands. After twelve years at Hammerton's, which Frank had transformed into an immensely profitable and expanding business, he took the opportunity to further strengthen his position within the company. A few years later the Hammerton family began to be concerned about losing complete control to Frank. They were also

Old photograph of Hammerton's brewery in Stockwell, since destroyed

being made very attractive offers for the business, so to the merry sound of money all round the association of Frank Rogerson with the brewing of beer in South London was ended.

Even before he left Hammerton's it seems that Frank was already interested in the burgeoning world of the London insurance market. He was a close friend and early business partner of Edward Mountain (1872-1948) the founder of Eagle Star Insurance. It seems that Frank Rogerson and his father Josiah (and maybe some of his brothers) had already helped set up or heavily invested in their own insurance company, called British Dominions General, which existed between 1904 and 1913. This was one of the core businesses from which Edward Mountain would acquire dozens of other companies to create Eagle Star. Edward Mountain was a financial genius, which was married to an uncanny intuition, which led him to refuse any business connected with the SS Titanic. Eagle Star advanced from marine into fire and then motor insurance, before expanding into life and commercial insurance over the 1920s and 1930s assisted by a confident, well-directed advertising campaign. Eagle Star would emerge as one of the

great financial institutions in the City of London, directed by three generations of the Mountain family. Edward Mountain was knighted in 1918 and made a baronet in 1922. His father had been a South London hop merchant known by two generations of Rogerson brewers. He had worked in that wonderful cast iron and glass marketplace that still stands in the heart of South London and had been able to afford to send his son Edward to Dulwich, to get a top-knotch education in one of South London's oldest public schools. Edward Mountain, just like Frank Rogerson, had gone straight from school into an apprenticeship, working as a trainee clerk in marine insurance. The two men could look each other in the eye. They were exactly the same age, with full knowledge of each-others' family, and they would stand at the altar and be godfathers to each-others children.

My knowledge of the actual figures are slight. The Rogerson family seem to have invested heavily (or partly owned) British Dominions General, which existed between 1904 and 1913 after which it became part of Eagle Star. Between 1913 and 1944 Frank Rogerson is listed as a Director of Eagle Star.

Defiance, the Ifracombe to Lynton stage coach, still in fine working order for the honeymoon of Frank Rogerson and Florence Allenby taken in the West Country, May 1896

Frank Rogerson, Director of Eagle Star Insurance

Mrs Frank Rogerson, Florence Allenby, as a widow, 1947

By 1920 Frank Rogerson was a wealthy man. When he had first started managing the Hammerton Brewery in 1894 he lived at 2 Stanfield Road, Stockwell – but within a year he felt secure enough to get married to his eighteen-year old sweetheart, Florence Allenby. It was a happy marriage though Florence was kept forever on the move, for Frank's flair for business was also exercised by the property market. He would pick up a house cheaply during a slump in trade at a cash price, restore it and then wait for the propitious moment to sell at a profit. He liked to move at least once every seven years. He was the seventh child and seven was his lucky number. His wife was kept happy by the progress into ever larger houses, with more servants and grounds. In 1901 they were living at 21 Sibella Road, Clapham, with two young children (Eve and Hugh); his young wife was assisted by Agnes Walsh, the Welsh cook and nanny Maud Eustace from Worcester. Later they moved to 12, Valley Road, Streatham with room for a resident cook and two parlour maids. From thence into a solid house, High Ridge on Downs Road which led up to the Derby racetrack on Epsom Down. In 1923 they moved to Chinthurst Hill, which was a very grand house, designed by Lutyens. It stood in its own grounds of 200 acres at Wonersh outside Guildford. Frank picked it up for £25,000 (about £ 1.5 million today) sold it for a

handsome profit six years later and then acquired a great gloomy gothic mansion called Fintry at Brook near Godalming in 1929. It later became, quite deservedly, a lunatic asylum. In 1935, as a speculation, he bought Red Court which stood on top of a hill outside Haslemere. It was set in its own grounds of a hundred acres with views over the South Downs. It was a light and elegant house

RedCourt in the snow

Fintry, Brook, Godalming, home between 1929–1935

with a handsome forecourt and eleven bedrooms. A stone fireplace dominated the entrance hall and two dozen could sit around the table in the dining room. There was an orangery where a door let you out into a circular loggia that overlooked the lawns and gardens, complete with grass tennis courts, paddocks, stables, woods and a large walled vegetable garden. There were cottages for the gardeners and a lodge house (for Reynolds the chauffeur) on the corner of the drive as it branched off from Scotland Lane. While they were there the property market slumped, much one suspects to Florence's relief, and so it became their home for fifteen whole years. Frank died in 1946 aged seventy-four. He was taken from home only six hours before his death, but even then managed to get a chuckle from his stretcher bearers, when he offered to swop places with one of them, who he thought didn't look that well himself.

Photograph of RedCourt, designed by Ernest Newton

Another holiday taken in Devon, Frank Rogerson outside Gare Manor, 1919

Frank Rogerson holding pale top hat in 1925 with his wife Florence (the larger of the two women)

Frank and Michael in Norway

Frank welcoming two of his brothers, possibly Jack and Charlie

Frank standing beside gate at RedCourt with two daughters-in-law, Marion and Gertie and wife Florence

CHAPTER EIGHT

Victorian Patriarch:
Josiah Rogerson (1832–1903)

To be ignorant of what occurred before you were born is to remain perpetually a child.
For what is the worth of a life unless it is woven with the life of our ancestors?
Cicero

Josiah William Stevens Rogerson (1832–1903) is the bearded man at the centre of the Victorian family photograph. He is the common ancestor of all the Rogerson cousins that I know about. He was born in Beccles in Suffolk and was only ten when his father, Charles Josiah Rogerson died. Josiah finished his schooling with two years at the Fauconberge Grammar School in Beccles (aged nine to eleven) then worked for a wine merchant friend of his father's before getting an apprenticeship in a brewery. This was the period when he courted, and (just twenty-four years old) married Lucy Maria Kettley, on 19 March 1856 at St Barnabas church, South Kennington. Her mother, another Lucy, was born in Great Ley in Essex around 1806. In the census of 1861 Josiah is listed as a Brewer's Clerk and was living at Chapel Hill with his wife and two young boys. Ten years later (aged thirty-nine) he is the Managing Director and Head Brewer of Christie's great brewery in Hoddesdon, Hertfordshire. It grew to become was one of the largest and most efficient breweries in England (supplying 159 tied public houses) as well as distilling its own brand of spirits. Long after Josiah retired, it was brought from the Christie family in 1927 by Taylor Walker's Cannon brewery.

Josiah lived straight across the road from the great brewery works in Myddleton House which may have been built for him (in 1852) on the site of the Queen's Head. Just a few yards down the High Street stood a pair of venerable coaching Inns. The Salisbury Arms stands opposite the Hoddesdon clock tower. It is still a mass of oak beams, complete with splendid old brick fireplaces and some surviving Elizabethan frescoes from when it was known as the Star before being renamed, the Black

Lion in 1578. It had the right to suspend its sign from a great single beam that stretched across the highway. This fell down in the storm of 1828, after which it changed its name again to the Salisbury Arms in a salute to the Cecil family who lived at Hatfield House. For all those centuries the inn had served as the traditional parliament of the maltsters of Hertfordshire after the Hoddeson market. The High Street was broad enough to become a market-place which divided this ancient old town into the rival parishes of Amwell and Broxbourne. The High Street became a meat market on Wednesday and a hop market on Thursdays. Hoddesdon (like the neighbouring town of Ware) was also known for malting, and the maltsters constructed ornamental booths at the end of their gardens, so that they could watch the barges carry the malt down the river Lea to the London breweries.

In its heyday Hoddesdon sat right astride the political nerve of England, a day's journey out of London on the coach road to Cambridge, with the rival inns kept busy by the thirty-five stage coaches that passed this road every day. A brick tower of Rye House still stands, which was the place where a plot was hatched to assassinate King Charles II (on his way to the Newmarket races) and where the Great Bed of Ware was displayed for many years. It is now in the Victoria and Albert museum.

In the census of 1861 we can read how Josiah's young family (and his old mother-in-law) were cared for by three live-in servants in Myddleton House, Amwell Street, Hoddesdon. (By some happy coincidence of names I live in a small London street that stands between Amwell street and Myddleton Square). Ten years later

VIEWS OF HODDESDON BREWERY.

The Brewery, Hoddesdon, Herts.

Hoddesdon Brewery owned by the Christie family who employed Josiah Rogerson as Managing Director and Head Brewer

(just before he was fifty) we can see the Rogerson household in even greater detail, with the names of a governess (Ada Bradley), a cook (Lucy Curieff), a maid (Lousia Clark) and a nursemaid (Ellen Aldridge). His large family is complete. By 1891 he had retired, quit Hertfordshire and went to live with his son Harry, his wife and his two daughters at a house on Alcester Road in Surrey.

Twelve years later he would leave his three eldest sons (John, Arthur and Charles) in charge of a trust worth £11,803 and 7 shillings for the care of their mother and their two sisters. Each son had been given an education, placed in an apprenticeship and a gold watch on their twenty-first birthday.

He has so many descendants that I have moved their stories to an appendix, The Cousinage.

View of a working brewery courtyard

Photograph of Brewery Dray

Dray in front of the Hoddesdon Brewery

CHAPTER NINE

Back to the Land

One can discourage too much history in one's family, but one cannot always prevent geography
Saki

Charles Josiah Rogerson (1801–1843) was the father of our Victorian patriarch Josiah. He inherited the tenancy of Barsham Hall but must have decided to sell, for there is a record of an auction of the farm stock in 1830. He would describe himself as a farmer for a few more years, possibly keeping hold of some aspect of the tenancy while he also tried to run a business or two in the local market town. Beccles is perched above the river Waveney, complete with its own dock, a small fishing fleet and a medieval church with a spire. It was then a town of a thousand houses, the seat of the County Quarter Sessions, but came especially alive for the weekly Friday market and the great cattle fair on Whitsun Monday. This animation was repeated with horse races at the end of September culminating in the annual horse fair on 2 October.

Charles Rogerson invested in an inn with its own brew house while also setting himself up as a tea merchant. In the census of 1841 we glimpse him listed as a 'Tea Dealer' living in Sheepgate Street with his household of children and a fifteen year old maidservant, Emily Barker. The tea trade had long been a monopoly of the East India Company, and traders had to attend the chaotically animated auctions by candlelight, though there was also illicit importation through Dutch merchants. In 1834 the tea trade had been opened up, and much more efficient and specialised auctions were held once a month in London's Mincing Lane. At this period China had a complete monopoly on tea (for the tea-garden-estates in Assam and Ceylon had not yet been planted) and the Chinese kept the fine details of the trade to themselves, consigning chests to the foreigners in such treaty ports as Canton. They kept the best tea for themselves and it was vital to inspect and sample each shipment imported, for trade labels

such as Bohea, Pekoe, Souchong, Soumlo and Hyson embraced all sorts of types and conditions. Maybe Charles Rogerson would have made a success of this venture but he died aged forty-two on 25 April 1843.

We have a documentary snapshot of his young family at his death (because his will survives) and we find them living in the centre of town at no 1, Blythburgate, a 17th century brick house with a pair of bow-windows on the first floor. Charles seems to have worked elsewhere, or perhaps during his last illness the family had to make some tough decisions, for the ground floor was rented out to James Feltham, a boot-maker. After his death Charles Rogerson's inherited portfolio of property holdings, a huddle of three tiny cottages in Burnham Overy Staithe (in North Norfolk), some property in the parish of St Giles in central Norwich (a yard and its surrounding tenements) and something in Kingston, Surrey, were all sold in order to buy a small street of a dozen rentable houses (later destroyed after the Second World War when it was listed as a depraved slum) to

Headstone of Charles Josiah Rogerson (father of Josiah) somewhere in Beccles graveyard

Barsham Hall, an imaginary view but showing its old relationship with the riverbank

Barsham church where farmer Thomas Rogerson (1757–1835) lies buried

support his widow and their four children. His widow, Mary Ann Rogerson (1798–1852) lived, gave birth and died in her hometown of Beccles. They were married 13 December 1825. I have tried to imagine her in the brick townhouse, No 46, Northgate Street, bustling through the streets, a figure on the edge of respectable gentility, but one that was yet supported from the rents of low-life in the mews-like property just a few streets away, known as Shaw's Yard. There is a tale that widow Rogerson needed little protection. She was a Ward (daughter of John Ward and Anne Parton), a Beccles-based clan whose activities over the generations had embraced smuggling and other maritime 'ventures'. Indeed it is rather to be feared that Mrs Rogerson's street of cottages became the town's red-light district. Nevertheless she put up a pious headstone to her husband in the Anglican Church graveyard, which I have looked for (having been sent a photograph), but never yet found. Her eldest son, William (baptised in 1831) stayed at home to look after his widowed mother and his two sisters. Ann (had been baptised in 1829) but Mary (the youngest of the family) who was born in 1840 would have barely remembered her father. William Rogerson is listed in the census as a merchant's clerk and seems to have stayed in town long enough to put up a headstone on his mother's grave. His presence permitted his younger brother, Josiah to leave town and make his own way in life.

Thomas Rogerson (1757-1835) was the father of Charles Josiah Rogerson. He was a Suffolk farmer who ended his days in Barsham Hall. He is the last outpost of the astonishing oral memory of Aunt Eve. In the pre-internet era, I could find no reference to anything about Barsham Hall anywhere and I am afraid rather lost confidence in this strand of Aunt Eve's storytelling. Decades later, I found a copy of his will, signed, sealed and dated.

Thomas Rogerson was the eldest child of William and Sarah Rogerson who had lived and farmed in Narborough. Thomas married Frances Baldwin (from St Giles in Norwich) in 1792 but his young wife died a year later, having given birth to a daughter, Frances. Thomas then married Sarah Garner who came from Thetford St Cuthbert. He seems to have inherited the copyhold leasehold of a farm in Narborough (a village just outside Swaffham in Norfolk) from his father. He served as the church warden there from 1784–91. This land would be valued for tax purposes at £133 13s. 4d. Later we find him in possession of Barsham Hall.

I invited myself to have coffee with the current owners of Barsham Hall. They had taken over the place in such disorder that they believed it must have remained unoccupied (apart from being used as a cowshed) since it was used as a barracks by Cromwell's soldiers in the Civil War. It is a moody old place, a barn-like manor house built over a Romano-British villa in the fourteenth century which Trollope combined with Roos Hall to make Carbury in, *The Way We Live Now*. Trollope sets much of the action of this great novel along the Wayeney valley and the two Suffolk market towns of Beccles and Bungay. He writes "the Carburys had been in Suffolk a great many years and had always held up their heads. But they had never held them very high." The Hall is surrounded by good farmland and though now enclosed by trees would in the old days have had a clear view, for just to the north the land drops down to the banks of the navigable River Waveney. After coffee I was walked to Barsham Church and introduced to a most hospitable deacon (who had inherited a farm in the parish). He kindly dug out some church records, so that I could see for myself that Thomas Rogerson had been buried in Barsham Church on 3 November 1835 at the ripe age of seventy-eight. The deacon had also remembered that his father's pigman (Henry Pipe) used to refer to 'Rogersons Pond' as a landmark when giving field directions. So I was taken on a muddy but fascinating walk up through what had been the three tenant farms of Marsh Farm, Laurels Farm and White House Farm which had once all been part of the Suckling Estate, established in 1615. We were joined by a young farmer who suggested that the pond had probably been dug to water cattle, or to soak flax for the making of linen. The pond was not pretty, full of rusting barbed wire and cow shit, but I was thrilled by an oral memory still echoing after two hundred years and recalling old farmer Rogerson. Then we had tea with a member of the Suckling family, which tied us up nicely with Nelson, whose mother Catherine Suckling was born in the Rectory. This proved to be the end of living history. I would find out a lot more, but it is archival research.

Narford Church, St Marys where farmer William Rogerson (1729–1785) served as Church Warden, he farmed in nearby Narborough

We discovered that Thomas Rogerson of Barsham Hall was the son of **William Rogerson** (1729-1785). William Rogerson held land in Narborough (probably as a copy-holding tenant farmer) and was listed as a church warden at Narford in 1761. He was baptised in 1729 and in 1753 married Sarah Halet (1729–1805) who came from Huntingfield. They had six surviving children. Thomas (our ancestor) was born in 1757, followed by a sister Sarah Rogerson (1761), who married Henry Hudson. Then there was another son, John Rogerson (1767), then another sister Elizabeth Rogerson (1769) who married John Baly in 1790. Then two more girls, Ellen Rogerson (1773) and Ann Rogerson (1774).

The father of William Rogerson was himself called William Rogerson. He had married his wife Mary Theoderik when she was just sixteen years old in 1718. Mary's Theoderik family had lived in Swaffham for many generations and her parents were called Thomas and Mary. I guessed she must have been pregnant, even before we found the records for their first-born child, Mary Rogerson – born in 1718. So it is likely that they were not married before the altar in the pomp of the vast cathedral-like nave of Swaffham's wool church but hurriedly by a young curate in the morning in the porch. After the birth of Mary there was a sorry succession of two Thomases and three Elizaes who were all born and then buried, between 1720 and 1726. We are not sure if any of these survived apart from our ancestor, William Rogerson born in 1729.

Since this William's grandfather was another William Rogerson, we have three farmer William Rogerson's in succession. This oldest of the three William Rogerson's farmed outside Swaffham. He had a daughter who married a Norfolk farmer William Rasbone (who farmed at East Rudham). His eldest son was called Thomas Rogerson who took over his father's farm at Swaffham. He was married to Elizabeth Haylett and they had four children: Anne Rogerson, Thomas Rogerson, William Rogerson and Elizabeth Rogerson. He makes his will out in 1734 and dies four years later in 1738. Thomas Rogerson was a prosperous man, able to leave between £400 and £200 pounds to each of his children, with a suggestion that he had already settled some money on his daughters at the time of their marriages, which would make each of

Swaffham Fair. William Rogerson married his pregnant teenage girlfriend (Mary Theoderik) in her hometown of Swaffham in 1718

his legacies exactly equal. These were very useful sums to inherit in the days when a vicars salary was £50 a year, a farm worker would receive £15 a year and a domestic servant less than £5. Thomas Rogerson was also trusted. He was chosen to be the executor for both his fathers will and that of a kinsman (Robert Goulty of Darsingham) who was another prosperous Norfolk farmer.

It seems likely that one of his two son's joined the Royal Navy but probably did not have any descendants for he died of fever in the West Indies as a young midshipman. His brother prospered, and we believe that one of his grandsons trained as a printer in Norwich and later became a publisher in London. This family story does not have any legal paperwork behind it, though I can remember my grandfather proudly pointing out a collection of half a dozen framed sporting prints and old bound volumes that bear the name of 'Rogerson & Tuxford' on the title page. Rogerson & Tuxford were printer-publishers working in the traditional London quarter for that trade which was in the alleys around Fleet Street. This had been the hive of the free press ever since Wynkyn

de Worde took over Caxton's Press and set up his print works in Fleet Street. The streets around St Paul's Cathedral were for many centuries the accepted centre for bookshops and book barrows. The core of Rogerson and Tuxford's business was a pair of energetic young barristers from the Inner Temple: Cuthbert Johnson and William Shaw. In 1832 they had set up *Mark Lane Express; Agricultural Journal and Livestock Record,* which campaigned for the security of tenant farmers along with agricultural improvements and education. Alongside their work as campaigning writers, William Shaw stood for parliament and was one of the founding figures of the Royal Agricultural Society in 1838 and the Farmers' Club in 1842. They were the bright lights. In the background, the working proprietors were John Rogerson and his son Joseph Rogerson, and their business partner George Tuxford. Other journals were later launched, such as *The Farmers Magazine, Ruff's Guide to the Turf, The Ladies Companion, The Sporting Review, The Sportsman* and *The New Sporting Magazine.* One of their most successful authors was Henry Hall Dixon, who wrote wittily on country sports. Other

Rogerson & Tuxford titles include *Silk and Scarlet* by the Druid, *Saddle & Sirloin*, *English Farm and Sporting Worthies* or *Tales and Traits of Sporting Life* by Henry Corbert. They also developed a useful line in selling sporting prints by artists such as Samuel and Henry Alken, who produced a stream of caricatures and etchings about steeple-chasing, racing, hunting and coaching.

John Rogerson was born in 1785 died on 11 May 1851. His son Joseph Rogerson carried on the business. From 1852–61 Rogerson & Tuxford were at 246 or 265 The Strand until 1877 after which they traded from 24, Norfolk Street, The Strand.

But enough of this branch of the family tree. We are descended from Thomas Rogerson's much less successful younger brother William Rogerson.

So to summarise after this distraction. We are all descended from Thomas Rogerson son of William Rogerson (1729-1785) son of William Rogerson (born 1702) son of William Rogerson (1669-1720). This oldest William Rogerson farmed outside Swaffham. He was baptised on 18 June

John Rogerson, the successful London Publisher is believed to be the grandson of the successful Thomas Rogerson who farmed outside Swaffham. We are all descended from Thomas's less capable younger brother, William.

1669, made out his will in 1717 and died in 1720. We do not yet know the name of his wife, but we can broaden out from these dry dates and look at the sort of life, that he, his children, his grandchildren and great grand-children lived. Four generations of Farmer Rogersons.

Throughout the seventeenth, eighteenth and nineteenth centuries all the great agricultural estates were divided up into tenant farms, usually between 100 and 400 acres in extent. There was a vast range in the size of the estates, for a great-coal mine-owning duke in the north of England might entertain a hundred tenant farmers to a Christmas feast in his castle while an old landed family on the coast of Suffolk might have just five farms and work the central one of these themselves as 'the home farm'. In theory the landlord held the whip hand over his tenant farmers, but in practice the odds could be tilted in the other direction. For the farmers, in the restricted franchise of those days, were an influential element in parliamentary elections, out of which landed families tried further to assert and enrich themselves. They usually wanted their tenant farmers loyal and on-side. Some of the tenant farmers were also copy-holders (in possession of ancient documents) which seems to have allowed their sons to inherit the tenancy. While knowledge of the land and the local climate – which fields flooded, which were prone to a last frost, which soils required a frequent dressing of lime or could be spoiled by deer coming out of the forest, which men in the village to employ (and which to avoid) – could take many years to acquire. Removing a tenant farmer and replacing him with a new man did not always benefit either a landlord or the land. Tenancies could be written to any legal shape but in East Anglia were usually for seven or fourteen years.

A lease-holding tenant farmer like William Rogerson would have employed about eighteen permanent workers who would have helped him work the land with a team of half a dozen horses. The most important manpower choices were made at the annual Michaelmas Fair (29 September)

where year-long contracts would be either renewed, or new men taken on. The three key workers on a farm where the teamsman (in charge of horses and the stables), the yardsmen (in charge of cattle) and the shepherd, who took care of the sheep. At critical periods of activity, extra labourers would be hired in as 'piece-workers' from the village or came as part of a contracted team of harvesters. Behind the row of harvesters with their scythes came a support team of women and boys. To rake the neat lines of cut wheat into 'gavel rows' and would then be gathered up and knotted into sheaves, brought together into a shock. Then it was the turn of the wagons to empty the fields, with the shocks pitch-forked up into towering ricks constructed on the wagons. These were carted to the farmyard, and either thatched against the weather or taken directly into the barns. Before the time of the mobile thresher (powered by a belt driven off a tractor engine) one of the worst jobs of the farming year was threshing in the dusty 'middlestead' of a barn, with the two double doors opened to encourage as much draft as possible. After the threshing had been achieved (achieved with a lethal looking flail in the old days), you needed a cross wind which would encourage the chaff to be blown down wind of the heavier grain as it was thrown up by wooden shovels into the air. The grain pile would later be sieved into hessian sacks, weighed and then sewn up, with all the chaff put aside as animal feed. This sacking process allowed for the harvest to be assessed, though it was traditional for the tithe to be taken off the field, with every tenth sheath put aside, which would be separately carted off to the Church barn.

I can remember my father, my uncles and my grandfather talking joyfully about such matters, their tales much enriched by the experience of the war years where old men came back to help on the farms. Strict rationing during the war years brought back all sorts of old machinery as well as stories of the old ways which were relished and remembered by the volunteers. Our weekly pocket money (a silver sixpence) was a reflection of this, for it was what a village boy would be paid for assisting with the harvest for six days. A 'boy' on a farm was anyone who remained at school or worked on a casual basis. He was promoted to 'lad' when he worked (or aspired to work) full-time on a farm. A lad would serve an apprenticeship, doing odd jobs for the teamsman,

the shepherd and the yardsmen, while he worked out what he did best. When he became useful at one of these tasks he would be paid a 'halfman's wage' before qualifying as a 'three-quarter man'. Once at that level it was usual practice to attempt to find your next promotion on a neighbouring farm.

The eigteenth-century was the heyday of the English tenant farmer, who stood mid-way in the social pecking order between the landlord in his country house and the labourer in the village. Ninety per cent of English land was managed under tenant farms, a vast social landscape formed from 15,000 villages and 5,000 estates. The tenant or yeoman farmer was the role model for John Bull, the national archetype of England, so beloved by the political cartoonists of the eigteenth-century – a stout, middle-aged, country-dwelling Anglo-Saxon, fond of strait speaking and passionate about liberty and beef. As Washington Irving described him,

> with much less of poetry about him than rich prose. There is little of romance in his nature, but a vast deal of a strong natural feeling. He excels in humour more than in wit; is jolly rather than gay; melancholy rather than morose; can easily be moved to a sudden tear or surprised into a broad laugh; but he loathes sentiment and has no turn for light pleasantry. He is a boon companion, if you allow him to have his humour and to talk about himself; and he will stand by a friend in a quarrel with life and purse at whatever the cost.

The King of England, George III, delighted in his nickname of 'farmer George', consciously dressed in the honest homespun cloth of England and liked to dine at home (at little expense), delighting to breakfast on a boiled egg from his own hens.

The enclosure acts had gradually transformed the vast open fields of medieval England (sub-divided into individual strips of ploughland and areas of common grazing) into a neat patchwork of fields that could reward the patient investment of labour. This led to the hedging and ditching of the land, in order to drain the fields and to allow herds to be folded on to selected fields for the richness of their manure. The application of marl explains the pattern of small quarry workings all over the chalkland, for this was quarried and then spread over fields which were too acidic. The practical suggestions for agricultural improvements (championed by such East Anglian farmer-landlords as Thomas Coke of Holkham, Arthur Young and Turnip Townshend) had effectively doubled crop yields over the eighteenth-century. Nor did these improvements require heavy investment, for the central platform of this Agricultural Revolution was a four-fold rotation of crops. Beet and turnips were to be followed the next year by barely, then clover and beans to prepare the ground for wheat in the fourth year. This rotation of crops could be pursued in different fields to keep the wheat-harvest money flowing, while herds could be fattened on the root crops. Between 1650 and 1850 the population of England trebled in size, keeping labour cheap and the markets hungry. Until 1760 the farmers of England could still expect to export some of the national harvest, but thereafter our island had to import corn to feed the ever more rapidly expanding population. It was a sad fact of rural economics that fat profits for farmers only came from other people's natural disasters. The difficult years of 1708 to 1710 drove wheat prices up by over 200% for those lucky enough to get a harvest in. On the other hand a series of good, bumper harvests always drove the work load up and the price right down. The French Revolutionary and the Napoleonic Wars meant a boom time for English farming which also helped push up the price of land. In 1812 a farmer could get 122 shillings for eight bushels of wheat (a quarter ton). The period of peace after Waterloo (1815–1837) however was effectively a long agricultural depression only partly mitigated by the unpopular Corn Laws, which attempted to stabilise the price on behalf of the farmers.

You can discover this world for yourself, if you read any of the novels of Henry Fielding, George Eliot, Jane Austen or Thomas Hardy. In the background to all these novels is the threat of a descent into the deprivation of the dark, unlit cottage of the English farm labourer, built chiefly from wood infilled with wattle and daub. There would be a brick-built fireplace in the principal ground-floor room where cooking in these cottages was done in the ashes of a wood fire. Such a cottage would often have just one upstairs bedroom which worked for all members of the household, and in winter families usually shared some or all of the ground floor with their animals. Water was fetched from a well, spring or stream, and manure heaps were squatted on in the morning. Milk could be drunk fresh if the family owned a cow but was mostly turned into butter and cheese which would not only keep but was a useful source of cash if sold at market. Weak ale was drunk in preference to dirty water by most members of the family, for tea would not become widely available until the middle of the nineteenth-century. Meals were based on bread, enlivened by soups and stews chiefly made from carrots, onions, peas, cabbage and potato. Meat predominately came to these pots in the form of household chickens or from the much-relished slaughter of a pig at the beginning of winter. Nothing of this animal would be wasted, let alone the blood (turned into black-pudding sausage), the skin (roasted to make crackling), the hooves (from which a rich jelly was extracted) and the fat which would be melted and hoarded to make dripping or as a baste for roasting vegetables. The Game Laws, including the prohibition of any hunting of any kind in the dark, effectively restricted shooting to those who owned land. So those harmless looking eighteenth-century sporting prints, have an imbedded element of class privilege.

The small farm-house where Jane Austen lived with her mother and sister, has survived. They were gentry but the big copper where the household linen was boiled in an out-house also doubled up as the butcher's basin where a slaughtered pig would have its bristles scalded off with boiling water. Jane shared a small bedroom with her sister all her life, and the quilt which warmed the bed took her years to make. The desk where her great novels were composed is a small table which would have been banged into, any time the door into every tiny family sitting room was opened. Some of the key indicators of this genteel life are almost invisible to our eyes, but villagers of the time would have noticed the dry brick walls, the wind-proof glass in all the windows and the oil lamps and candles that allowed for reading in the evening. The greater heat of a coal fire lit in a cast-iron grate and a kitchen kept within its own separate room would remain a mark of privilege into the mid nineteenth-century. The tea that was served in china, the wine that was poured into a glass, the books bound in leather and the oil paintings on the walls were other key elements of a prosperous home – and ones which we can still recognise. This was a lifestyle that could be maintained by tradesmen in a county market town, by clergymen and tenant farmers.

Furniture in cottage, farmhouse and modest town house would have been sparse, made out of wood by craftsmen in the local market town and would have looked by our standards rather spartan, with none of the upholstered armchairs and sofas that we all sprawl upon today.

CHAPTER TEN

The Denton & Dublin Connection
Revd Robert Rogerson & Sir John Rogerson

He who has no fools, knaves or beggars in his family was begot by a flash of lightning.
Thomas Fuller

We have established that **William Rogerson** (1669-1720) a tenant farmer at Swaffham is the oldest ancestor we can be certain of in terms of a well-documented trail of birth, marriage, death certificates and wills. At this remove, he is already just one of five hundred and twelve equally relevant genetic ancestors from that single generation. We could stop here, and there is good reason to, for should you meet them in the place beyond, you could look all these ancestors in the eye and shake them firmly by the hand. But there is a long tradition that we are descended from the Rogerson's buried in Denton church on the border of Suffolk and Norfolk. There is a whiff of sulphur about some of these men but the story of our connection with them is too old to ignore, and there are some interesting tales that unfold. All the three members of the Rogerson family interested in their story, cousin Phyllis, Aunt Eve and Sydney Rogerson all believed this. I was also intrigued to spot that a generation further back from them, my great-great uncle the Revd Arthur Rogerson had named his house in Sussex, 'Denton.' Yet another salute to this long-remembered connection, though the actual links in the chain had been forgotten.

I believe that William Rogerson (1669-1720) was the eighth child of The Revd Robert Rogerson (vicar of Denton). We know that Robert and his wife Barbara had a son called William who was born in 1669. This is itself not proof-positive but is an undeniably neat fit, like the moment you join two separate bits of a jigsaw puzzle together. There was no way of being absolutely certain that we had positively found this missing link in the chain. To reduce the odds, my father and I had all the surrounding Suffolk and Norfolk parish registers checked, in an ever-widening geographical circle. Before the days of genealogical websites this was laborious, but seemed worthwhile, just in case there were lots of other Rogerson families nearby, also giving birth to boys called William in 1669. We used a researcher who found no evidence of any other Rogerson family in the region, let alone

Denton Church. It is long been understood that we are descended from the Rogersons buried in this church, but no-one could remember exactly how.

another William Rogerson. All we found was one large Rogerson family at Denton, the children of the Revd Robert Rogerson and Barbara Gooch. (Thomas Rogerson was baptised 30 June 1661, Anna Rogerson baptised 7 September 1662, a second Anna Rogerson baptised on 21 Sept 1663, Margaret Rogerson on 24 August 1664, John Rogerson on 9 January 1665, Charles Rogerson on 19 Nov 1666, Elizabeth Rogerson on 13 January 1667, William Rogerson on 18 June 1669, Barbara Rogerson on 31 March 1672 and Robert Rogerson on 31 March 1673.

There is however one other problem that needs addressing, for the handsome tomb of Rev Robert Rogerson in Denton church does not mention William among his four living children, but that may yet be explainable if he had been cast out from his family. I can certainly think of similar tales from each generation of our family. This is all guess work, but William Rogerson may have behaved just like one of his own sons and got a local girl pregnant before she was seventeen. Perhaps she worked in the house, and he had been expelled from his father's household for not confessing any guilt, quite aside from the issue of marrying her, or not marrying her.

He would not become a gentleman like his brothers but would descend to the next step down in class, a tenant farmer. As we will find out, he would not have been alone, as many of the other male children of the Revd Robert Rogerson were in some way disowned or decided to emigrate.

The Revd Robert Rogerson (1627-1714) was a proud and ambitious man, who had survived three political upheavals in the English Civil War, the Cromwellian Commonwealth and the Stuart Restoration with his status growing with every passing year. The sudden rise to great fortune of his young cousin, Sir John Rogerson (1648-1724), the Lord Mayor of Dublin, must have further spurred on his social ambitions. He would also watch his wife's young nephews (William Gooch and Thomas Gooch) on the first steps of their public careers, which would take them to the very summit of English society. He died in 1714 before they had quite made it to the top.

These two nephews were a remarkable pair of men. William Gooch (1681–1751) was born in Great Yarmouth. He served as a soldier under John Churchill in his brilliant campaigns in the Low Countries, then under Admiral Vernon in

Rogerson and Gooch arms above one of the tombs in Denton church

the West Indies. In 1727 he was made Royal Lieutenant-Governor of Virginia and enforced the Tobacco Inspection Act of 1630, which made planters transport their crops to public warehouses where they were inspected, stored and categorised. This quality control worked its magic and allowed the world to fall in love with 'The Finest Virginia'. William made a formal peace with the Six Nations (a confederation of Native American tribes) and received their permission to settle the Shenandoah valley. William was a firm upholder of the Church of England, but he also understood political realities, so he encouraged the Presbyterians within Virginia to settle the Shenandoah valley and make it their own. There is also a happy story of William refusing to ignore the incipient racism of colonial society, and insisting on raising his hat to a woman, whatever her colour or legal status. In 1746 he was made a baronet and a major general the following year. In 1749 he returned to England, though not before he and his wife had buried their fondest hopes for the future, for their twenty-six year old son William (who was serving in the Royal Navy) had expired of the bloody flux. Staunton in Virginia was named after the maiden name of

William's wife Rebecca and Goochland county for himself. He died in London in 1751, but by special dispensation his baronetcy was permitted to pass to his younger brother. Thomas Gooch had become chaplain to Queen Caroline, George II's clever wife, who corresponded with philosophers, supported the work of Handel, designed Hyde and Green Park and concerned herself with the Church of England. Thomas was part of this uniquely intellectual royal court. He married three times and become notorious as the worldly Bishop of Bristol, Ely and Norwich. Thomas would survive at least one assassination attempt, inherit his brother's baronetcy and amass a fortune, some of which he passed onto Gaius, his old Cambridge college. He was a bit of an old villain, so I was delighted to discover that he is an ancestor of my wife.

The Rev Robert Rogerson may not have been a lovable figure but he was undoubtedly a plucky survivor, who had to chart his own way through an extremely tricky political period. He went up to university (Caius College, Cambridge) in 1645, right in the middle of the English Civil War and was ordained the year that King Charles I was executed (1649). It was a period in which you had to

Denton Rectory in its 18th century heyday with the powerful Bishop-Baronet Sir Thomas Gooch (chaplain to Queen Caroline) arriving by coach to visit his Rogerson relatives in the vicarage.

Sir Thomas Gooch, thrice bishop, thrice married who survived at least one assassination attempt. The nephew of Barbara Gooch, wife of The Revd Robert Rogerson of Denton

keep your own counsel and stay silent. East Anglia together with Cambridge compromised one of the heartlands of the Parliamentary party and the New Model army created by men such as Oliver Cromwell. Robert's father was an Anglican vicar who had been implicated as an obedient follower of the high church Anglican movement of King Charles I and Archbishop Laud, who were the arch villains of that period. For Robert's father (the Revd Thomas Rogerson) had caused a riot in his parish when he tried to enforce Archbishop Laud's reforms (such as reinstating an altar-like communion table draped in linen in the eastern apse framed off from the rest of the nave by wooden railings). So at the earliest opportunity he was 'sequestered' – thrown out of his vicarage by the Puritan party in his parish and forced to live as a penniless internal exile, taking shelter with a poor shepherd in his hut hidden away on some heathland. This happened right at the start of the Civil War in 1642. Yet three years later his son Robert was studying at Cambridge. We do not know who helped him out, though one might guess that it was probably the family of his great-uncle,

the Revd Christopher Rogerson. Robert Rogerson would also accept his first Church appointment in 1650 which was during the reign of Oliver Cromwell. This was the period when you would not have recognised the Church of England as we know it, for bishops had been formally abolished and cathedrals had been desecrated. The Church had become Presbyterian and was run by committees of Puritans. Robert would later claim that he had been ordained by a proper Anglican Bishop, Robert Maxwell, the Anglo-Irish Bishop of Kilmore, but if this did indeed happen at this time, he would have most certainly kept this fact to himself. Throughout the Cromwellian Commonwealth the Revd Robert Rogerson would be employed as a Church minister at Ormesby – just north of the busy port of Great Yarmouth, between the years 1650-59. He would have had to appear to have been a loyal Presbyterian to have been given such a post. But he clearly also maintained some important connection with the Cavalier faction, for even before King Charles II returned to England, the Rev Robert Rogerson has been presented the living of Denton by Henry Howard, second son of Lord Arundel. He was then in a position to marry Barbara Gooch, who came from a well-connected, land-owning family in Suffolk with trading interests in Great Yarmouth. Together they built the splendid Rectory in Denton with a walled garden and could afford to keep their own coach with four horses. That is very opulent behaviour for the vicar of a Norfolk village, especially one whose father had lived in abject poverty on a heath. An oil painting of their handsome house and garden (as lived in by their descendants in 1745) survives. They have nine children together before Barbara dies giving birth in 1684.

We do not know what happened to all of Robert and Barbara's children. Their eldest son Thomas Rogerson had been named after his paternal grandfather, the Revd Thomas Rogerson. Thomas was trained up as his father's clerical heir. He was appointed the vicar of Ampton in Suffolk as an apprenticeship but it was clearly intended that he would succeed to the now rather splendid Rectory at Denton. But the young Revd Thomas Rogerson had a crisis of conscience. He could not accept the Glorious Revolution (when Roman Catholic James II was swapped for his Protestant nephew William of Orange). Thomas Rogerson believed that an oath of loyalty once made to your monarch could never be changed. He became what was known as a non-juror and resigned rather than give a new oath of loyalty to William and Mary. About ten per cent of the clergy of England found themselves in this position. This act of high conscience infuriated his old father, who turned his back on his son. This rupture was observed by another cleric who wrote in his memoirs, 'Robert Rogerson kept a coach and four…He had a son, a non-juror, a character much more to be shunned that a leper with persons of Old Rogersons way of thinking, and he shunned his poor son accordingly." As we have seen, Robert had to negotiate half a dozen such political changes in order to have survived. So he spurned, then disinherited Thomas Rogerson, and selected the husband of his youngest daughter Elisabeth (the Revd Mathew Postlethwaite) as his chosen heir to the Rectory of Denton.

From this marriage descend a line of scholarly vicars of Denton, culminating in the **Thomas Kerrick** (1748-1828). He is a distant relative, but undoubtedly the finest artist connected with the Rogerson family. Thomas was a passionate antiquarian with the skill of a painter and an architectural draughtsman. He was also a miniature-painter, a practised etcher and one of the earliest lithographers. He contributed some drawings to Gough's *Sepulchral Monuments* and created the portraits of Henry VI and Richard III for Fenn's *Paston Letters*. He bequeathed his collection of early royal portraits to the Society of Antiquaries and gave to the British Museum his manuscript collections and sketches in illustration of ancient costumes, consisting chiefly of drawings from monuments, sepulchral brasses, stained windows, seals, armour, ecclesiastical buildings, and English castles and camps. These are contained in forty-eight volumes of various sizes. His son presented his father's large collection of coins to the Society of Antiquaries, and also bequeathed to the Fitzwilliam Museum at Cambridge seven pictures, two hundred books, and many valuable portfolios of early prints. Thomas was born 4 February 1748, the son of Samuel Kerrich, vicar of Dersingham and rector of Wolferton and West Newton, Norfolk, by his second wife, Barbara who was the elder daughter of Matthew Postlethwaite, archdeacon of Norwich, and the grandson of Barbara Gooch and the Revd Robert Rogerson. Thomas was educated

at Magdalene College, Cambridge and graduated in 1771, after which he was awarded a travel scholarship. Kerrich was accompanied by a pupil, John Pettiward, and they journeyed on their Grand Tour through France, the Low Countries, and Italy, living in Paris for six months and at Rome for two years where they made a fine collection of drawings of old monuments. Returning to Cambridge in 1775, Thomas received his M.A, after which he was elected a fellow of his college. In 1784 he was presented to the living of Dersingham, which had previously been held by his father; later topped up by the living of Hemisby, Norfolk, in 1786. In 1797 he was elected principal librarian of Cambridge University as well as being made a fellow of the Society of Antiquaries of London. He was later made a Prebend of Lincoln in 1798, and also of Wells in 1812. He married Sophia who was the daughter of Richard Hanyles, a Cambridge doctor and they had a son and two daughters. Thomas died at home on Free School Lane, Cambridge, on 10 May 1828.

This period, of the halcyon days of the eighteenth-century gentleman-scholar cleric has been brought alive in a small book, "*Your*

Thomas Batoni portrait of the young artist Thomas Kerrick (1748–1828) when on scholarship in Rome

Affectionate and Loving Sister" which is the edited correspondence between Barbara Kerrich and Elizabeth Postlethwaite (between 1733-51). They were sisters, the two daughters of Elizabeth Rogerson, the chosen heir of the Revd Robert and Barbara Rogerson. I found this book fascinating for it throws light on the sudden shifts in fortune that could transform a privileged life into desperate poverty. For on the death of one of their husbands (an outwardly jovial and confident Anglican vicar) a debt that has been hidden is suddenly exposed. We never get to know the cause of this debt, which could have been just the high living enjoyed by all students in their reckless youth. However, with no regular income to service the interest on this debt, everything has to be sold. The widow watches all her cherished possessions: furniture, ceramics and silver, auctioned off in an attempt to pay off the debt and is forced to retreat to live in a single attic room in Norwich which she occupies with her daughters.

The Revd Thomas Rogerson, the non-juror disinherited by his father, left a trust to be supplied by the rent of a pocket of fields, the Heigh Close (6 acres) and the Middle Close (3 acres), specified in a will dated 24 December 1722. This land had been purchased from Robert Snell from the village of Denton. The annual rent produced about ten guineas (£10.10s.). For many years £8 8s. was paid to a schoolmistress, who kept school in a house provided by herself, and as many children as were appointed by the rector, being all the poor children of the parish who offered themselves, and taught them reading and writing and the girls needle-work. The remaining £2 2s. was applied (at 10s 6d every quarter) in a distribution of sixpenny and threepenny loaves among poor persons who were regular attendants at church, the larger quantity being given to those who are in most regular attendance, and had the largest families to maintain. Two hundred and fifty years later, on the occasion of the millennium, a portion of the lands from this long defunct local charity was planted as Rogerson Wood, a little neighbourhood park for the village of Denton.

The Revd Robert Rogerson's youngest son, Robert Rogerson escaped from his father to the sea. He married Anne Courts in the wicked old city of Portsmouth in 1705 and would ultimately migrate to Virginia. Here his family would prosper and multiply, but they also kept hold of a limited portfolio of Rogerson given names: Thomas, John and Robert. We know this because one his descendants fought in the First World War and accidentally meet up with his distant English cousins.

The young cousin of the Revd Robert Rogerson who did so well for himself in Dublin was called John Rogerson (1648–1724). He was born in Holland (so was almost certainly the child of an exiled cavalier), which gave me a shiver of pleasure in case his life ties in with Aunt Eve's mythical tale. John Rogerson enjoyed a breath-taking rise to power, wealth and position in Restoration Ireland, as a merchant ship-owner and property developer with interests in both London and Dublin. His London-born wife Elizabeth Proby must have helped, if only through her connections. Elizabeth came from a well-known family immersed in the affairs of the City of London. Sir Peter Proby (a Lord Mayor of London) was her paternal grandfather and John Bland (another powerful London merchant) was her maternal grandfather.

In 1674 John and Elizabeth Rogerson were living in Dublin and attending the Protestant church of St Andrews off Dame Street in Dublin. But three years later 'She departed this mortal life the 10 November and was buried the 13 of the same month in St Bride's Church, Dublin 1677.' John Rogerson was made Alderman for life in 1683, Lord Mayor of Dublin in 1684, then became M.P. for Dublin in 1695, then Sheriff in 1707. He received the commission to construct a new harbour for the city of Dublin, still remembered in Sir John Rogerson Quay, and a whole block of usefully reclaimed land. He built Glasnevin House, which is now rather obscured by utilitarian additions built by the Roman Catholic Church, but does retain some magnificent baroque plasterwork in some of the surviving interior rooms. John Rogerson was knighted in 1693, taking the same coat of arms that the Revd Robert Rogerson used when they were buried inside Denton church. Who borrowed from whom? Or were they both aware of a shared tradition that has become lost to us? Is the prominent fleur de lys, a remnant memory of the Rogerson clan of Free French merchants on the Suffolk coast? We do not know.

They had three children, including John Rogerson (1676–1741) who became Attorney General then Lord Chief Justice of Ireland. This second, high-achieving John Rogerson married Elizabeth Ludlow, niece of Cromwell's murderously efficient right-hand hatchet man – a man whose name is still accursed throughout Ireland. The Rogerson land-holdings had now become especially valuable in the rapidly expanding cities of Dublin and Cork. There was a third generation John Rogerson but he was not a breeder. He died as a sixty-six-years old bachelor in 1785 and left all his money to specifically Protestant charitable schools. He sounds a prig. His sisters (Hannah Rogerson, Elizabeth Rogerson, Frances Rogerson and Arabella Rogerson) are not included in their brother's will. They appear much more lively characters. They all had colossal dowries (of £5,000 each on their wedding day) augmented by later inheritances of land which helped bump up their husbands in rank. So Arabella Rogerson and her husband James Cotter established the Cotter-Rogerson line of Baronets, Elizabeth Rogerson's husband Abraham Creighton became Lord Erne of Crom Castle, Hannah Rogerson married Anthony Norreys-Jephson (an M.P.) and Frances Rogerson married Robert Leslie of Glaslough. The descendants of all these four Rogerson women survived and bred to create a dense tapestry of Anglo-Irish landed families, assisted coats of arms, portraits, titles and great houses. I bump into some of their names, such as Molyneux and Cotter-Rogerson through my mother's own Anglo-Irish family. It is almost a harmless sport, tracing these names on to a chart but if you do so, it is useful to remind oneself that William Rogerson, a humble tenant farmer from the Norfolk town of Swaffham, is the oldest ancestor we can be certain of in the terms of a well-documented trail of birth, marriage, death certificates and wills. As we have already heard, he is genetically remote enough, and just one of 512 equally relevant ancestors of that generation. The relationship between the Revd Robert Rogerson and Sir John Rogerson was probably that of a second cousin. The Civil Wars created many breaks in the otherwise amazingly intact documentary records of the Church of England.

Let us return to the documented facts about the Revd Robert Rogerson. He was born on 4 June 1627 at Norton Subcarse, Norfolk, where his father served as vicar. He was actually baptised 'Robertus' in the parish register and had a younger sister called Margareta Rogerson who was born in 1631. He was schooled at Wymondham under Mr Wildman and at Norwich under Mr Lovering and then studied at Gaius College, Cambridge from 1645-8. As we have heard he was ordained a priest in 1649 after which he was appointed minister of St Margaret's at Ormesby. It was a useful first step on the clerical ladder, with a living worth £40 a year. In 1659 he was made Rector of Denton, presented with the living by Henry Howard, second son of Lord Arundel. He married Barbara Gooch at Denton after taking up this living. She had been born in 1637 and died 1684. He served as vicar of Denton for fifty-five years, during the reigns of five monarchs and died in 1714 with his will proved in 1715.

His father was the **Revd Thomas Rogerson,** (1595-1663). He was also educated at Caius College, receiving his degree in 1618 and then serving as a curate at Norton Subcarse in 1620, then the curate of Raveningham before being appointed Rector of Monk Soham in 1631. As we have already heard, his attempts to impose the Laudian reforms (the High Church party within the Church of England) in his parish caused a riot, led by the Puritan Wheymonde family who were probably influential in expelling him during the second year of the Civil War. He and his wife Margaret 'lived with a countryman in a very mean cottage upon a heath for some years, and in a very low and miserable condition.'

In 1646 a more moderate mood briefly reigned (Parliament was winning the war and Cromwell's New Model Army had not yet seized power). The inhabitants of Monk Soham petitioned The Committee for Plundered Ministers on behalf of their impoverished priest, Thomas Rogerson.

'Never having given any just scandal in his life, but orthodox in doctrine and of an honest, godly conversation…He has never done anything, to any of our knowledge in opposition to any of parliaments ordnances. We conceive him a very fit object, for the due consideration of the noble committee to restore him to his living of Munkes Soham, he being a man of learning and abilities and fit to discharge the duty of that place.'"

Interior of Monk Soham where The Rev Thomas Rogerson (father of Robert Rogerson) was expelled from his parish by Puritans during the Civil War

Worn pews within Monk Soham

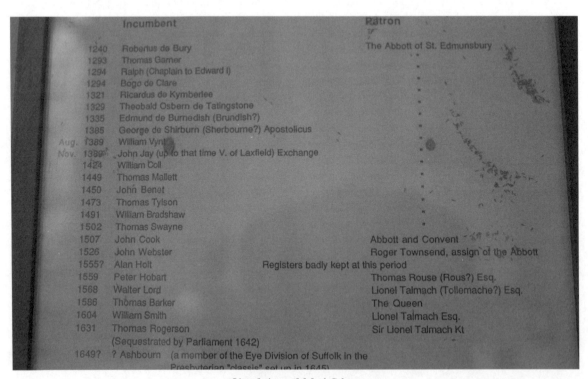

	Incumbent	Patron
1240	Robertus de Bury	The Abbott of St. Edmunsbury
1293	Thomas Gamer	
1294	Ralph (Chaplain to Edward I)	
1294	Bogo de Clare	
1321	Ricardus de Kymberlee	
1329	Theobald Osbern de Tatingstone	
1335	Edmund de Burnedish (Brundish?)	
1385	George de Shirburn (Sherbourne?) Apostolicus	
Aug. 1389	William Vynt	
Nov. 1389	John Jay (up to that time V. of Laxfield) Exchange	
1424	William Coll	
1449	Thomas Mallett	
1450	John Benet	
1473	Thomas Tylson	
1491	William Bradshaw	
1502	Thomas Swayne	
1507	John Cook	Abbott and Convent
1526	John Webster	Roger Townsend, assign of the Abbott
1555?	Alan Holt	Registers badly kept at this period
1559	Peter Hobart	Thomas Rouse (Rous?) Esq.
1568	Walter Lord	Lionel Talmach (Tollemache?) Esq.
1586	Thomas Barker	The Queen
1604	William Smith	Lionel Talmach Esq.
1631	Thomas Rogerson	Sir Lionel Talmach Kt
	(Sequestrated by Parliament 1642)	
1649?	? Ashbourn (a member of the Eye Division of Suffolk in the Presbyterian "classis" set up in 1645)	

List of vicars of Monk Soham

This petition was dated 9 July 1646 and was signed by twenty-two inhabitants of the parish, by eight clergyman and five others. Even the acting minister offered to vacate the rectory, for, 'I confess that I have been the Willinger to make this certificate because I heard some who were the chief means of putting him out, to say that he was prosecuted out of malice and I do believe it.' This little window on to the past is quoted from *The Puritans in Power* by G.B.Tatham. But the appeal was not effective, and the spirit of faction was such that at the Restoration one of the well-meaning clerical witnesses to this petition on behalf of Thomas Rogerson was himself ejected.

This Rev Thomas Rogerson was one of the eight children of the **Revd John Rogerson** (1571-1633) and **Anne Vyncent.** John Rogerson was vicar of Honingham from 1592–1633. He was married to Anne at Honingham on 23 April 1594 and their son Thomas was born the next year. Christopher, their second child, was born in 1597 followed by Elizabeth Rogerson (1599), George Rogerson (1602) and James Rogerson (1607). Christopher Rogerson was educated at Caius College, Cambridge (getting his degree in 1620) after which he worked as a curate at Natley before taking over as vicar of Honingham from his father in 1634. Christopher's own children appear to have been taken home to be baptised at his father's church at Honingham. This family included John Rogerson (1620), Thomas Rogerson (23 April 1622), Joseph Rogerson (16 February 1623), Kate Rogerson (13 August 1626) and Francis Rogerson (25 June 1628). So with two generations of Rogerson's baptised at the font of Honingham church there are plenty of candidates to fulfil Aunt Eve's exotic tale of a young exiled cavalier in Holland. I have some whisper of a memory that Francis was his name and that he was the father of John Rogerson. Honingham is about eight miles outside of Norwich, a sleepy hamlet, one of the 15,000 parishes of England.

There are traces of other Rogerson families from this period in Norfolk, notably a priest called John Rogerson of Roughton, son and heir of his father John Rogerson who was involved in a court case in Chancery in 1533-8 over some land outside Swaffham. There are also some familiar given names, such as William, son of John Rogerson born in Beeston-Next-Mileham (an obscure hamlet south of Fakenham) in 1559 and Thomas Rogerson, son of John Rogerson, born in 1550 in Holm Hale (another obscure hamlet, five miles east of Swaffham).

What has always attracted my interest is the horrible fate meted out to Ralph Rogerson, a tenant farmer on the lands of the Abbey of Walsingham. There had been a petition King Henry VIII to spare the Abbey of Walsingham which was one of the national shrines of England dedicated to an apparition of the Mother of God. This humble petition was distorted by the Court into a rebellion. In 1537, Henry was informed of 'a great insurrection like to be at Walsingham' by one his confidential agents listening to farmers talking in a pub, complaining that 'You see how the Abbeys go down, and our living goeth away with them.' Within a week, he had ordered the immediate execution of all who were involved in what he was pleased to call, 'The Walsingham Conspiracy'.

On 24 May 1537, a Royal Commission at Norwich Castle condemned eleven of those famers to be drawn, hung, beheaded, and then quartered for high treason. Two days later Ralph Rogerson, Thomas Howse, Richard Hendley, Thomas Menal and Andrew Pax were executed in the Castle Ditch. John Semblye and John Sellers were taken to Yarmouth to be killed on 28 May. Nicholas Mileham, the Sub-Prior of the Abbey, and George Gysborough, a layman, were put to death before the Abbey gates, on 30 May, and William Gysborough, who was apparently guilty of nothing worse than being brother to a conspirator, was hanged with John Pecock, clerk, in Lynn, on 1 June. This is not yet part of our story, though I like the idea that there is more work to be done for some future historian of the Rogerson family.

Our family story begins with three generations of Church of England vicars in Norfolk (John, Thomas, Robert), followed by four generations of Farmers in Suffolk (that succession of three William Rogersons all dutifully serving as church wardens in their villages) ending up with Thomas Rogerson at Barsham Hall. Then the move off the land by his son Charles Josiah Rogerson who becomes a Tea merchant in Beccles before dying quite young. His second son, Josiah Rogerson became the Master Brewer at Hoddesdon and placed six of his sons in the craft all over southern

William Gooch father of Barbara, died 1684 –
hung in Mettingham House until 1980

Sir William Gooch, the other successful nephew of Barbara
Gooch and the Rev Robert Rogerson

Elizabeth Buspole, married to William Gooch,
parents of Barbara Gooch

Sir John Rogerson (1648–1724) variously Lord Mayor,
M.P. and High Sheriff of Dublin and father of John
Rogerson (1646-1741) Lord Chief Justice of Ireland. He is
fascinating character. He is not an ancestor but a kinsman.

England. Two would become vicars in the Church of England. The Rogerson family maintains this link with brewing beer and malting barley for four generations, only ended comparatively recently with the deaths of Barry Rogerson in Hertfordshire and Gordon Cunliffe Rogerson in Suffolk. But new traditions have emerged. Three generations of Rogerson men have served as headmasters of Cottesmore, three generations of women have won the Newmarket Town Plate and three men have served as Commander Rogerson in the Royal Navy. You can also draw other lines, such as the entrepreneurial flair that connects Frank Rogerson with Nico Rogerson and with my brother James Rogerson. There are also three writers in the family. There are also three writers in the family, but if I had to put my finger on what makes a typical Rogerson, it would be their joy in a fully lived physical life rather than any soulful introspection, combined with a delight in drink and gardens, the company of their dogs, horses and children (in that order of affection) all washed over with a healthy irreverent laughter that makes them good company. Now and then you catch a glint of steel well-hidden beneath easygoing manners.

The Cousinage

If you don't know your history, you are a leaf that doesn't know that it is part of a tree
Michael Crichton

This chapter lists the descendants of the nine children of Josiah and Lucy Rogerson. One of the risks of setting yourself up as a family historian is that you can be taken to task over an incorrect birthday and or a misspelt middle name. My hope is that the many omissions of this book will inspire my cousins to write up their own misadventures.

The Revd Arthur William Rogerson was the eldest child of Josiah Rogerson, born 30 August 1859. He married Elizabeth (born in Hertford) and ran a brewery in that attractive old Sussex town of Lewes before becoming a vicar like his brother and his Norfolk ancestors. The census of 1911 catches him in a house on the Avenue named Denton filled with 3 grown up children and 3 servants. There he died in 1931.

Josiah Rogerson with Lucy-Maria and their nine children: back row from left, Arthur, Mini, Louisa, Jack; middle row from left Charlie, Josiah, Lucy-Maria, Sidney; bottom row from left Frank, Herbert, Harry.

They had five children: Arthur Percy Rogerson (born 1885), Cecil J. Rogerson (1887-1936), Ernest S. Rogerson (born 1889), Grace Rogerson (born 1882) and Constance Rogerson (born 1894). I think Grace married Lionel Johnson. Ernest served as a captain in the Royal Sussex Regiment and died in the fighting at Guillemont on 19 August 1916. Cecil worked as a doctor, first in Canterbury and then in Norfolk, where he died in 1936. Arthur Percy Rogerson worked at a brewery in Wokingham, Berkshire, after which he moved to Portsmouth where he died in 1919, one of the many victims of the Spanish Flu.

John William Rogerson 'Uncle Jack' was born 14 April 1860. He has his arms firmly crossed in the family photograph. He became a master brewer, then joint managing director of W. & G. Bartram Ltd, the Bridge Brewery, High Street, Tonbridge, Kent. It was a model family-owned, local brewery with fifty-one tied public houses in the neighbourhood. In 1911 he had moved and became a director of the Shalimar brewery on the Banstead Road in Epsom, Surrey. His household held two children, three servants, nursemaid Florence and Sybil the governess. John's wife was Louise Egerton Cunliffe, the Indian-born (at Thelum) daughter of Major-General Gordon Cunliffe and the niece of Major-General Sir Richard Cunliffe. I remember hearing about their cousin Bob Cunliffe from my grandfather for he was captain of the Royal Navy cricket team before the Second World War and served as captain of Dartmouth Royal Naval College after it. Louise gave birth to three children: Violet Rogerson, Gordon Rogerson and Barbara Rogerson.

Violet Rogerson married a stockbroker (L. Cox) and lived a comfortable and race-attending existence with her cousins. She died in 1986 but had no children. Her sister, Barbara Rogerson was married at least twice and had a number of daughters but, she, like many a self-willed soul disappeared off the kinship map, labelled a 'Black Sheep'. One longs to know more. Gordon Cunliffe Rogerson was born 25 February 1910 and followed the family inclination by working as a brewer, first in West London and then in Cheshire. His and his wife Nora Harvey-Boots (married in 1932) had three children, born during the 1930's: Michael, Timothy and John. Gordon retired to Suffolk and died in 1979, aged 69.

TONBRIDGE.

MARRIAGE OF MR. J. W. ROGERSON.

Under the very happiest auspices, the marriage took place on Wednesday, in London, of our genial and popular townsman Mr. John Williams Rogerson, joint managing director with Mr. R. H. Bartram of the important firm of W. and G. Bartram, Limited. Mr. Rogerson's bride was Miss Louise Egerton Cunliffe, of The Lodge, Bloxworth, Wareham, Dorset, youngest daughter of Major-General G. Gordon Cunliffe, late of the Bengal Staff Corps, a niece of Sir Robert Cunliffe, and cousin to the Oxford bowler, Mr. F. Cunliffe. The wedding was celebrated, with a full choral service, at the well-known West-End Church of the Hon. and Rev. Edward Carr-Glyn, St. Mary Abbott's, Kensington, the officiating clergymen being the Rev. Sidney Rogerson, M.A. (brother of the bridegroom), and the Rev. A. E. Farrat (nephew of Dean Farrar, and a life-long friend of the bridegroom's). The bride, who was escorted to the church and given away by her father, was attended by four bridesmaids—Miss May and Miss Ethel Cunliffe (her sisters), Miss Lane (her cousin), and Miss Lucy Rogerson (sister of the bridegroom); while the bridegroom's brother, Mr. Herbert P. Rogerson, acted as best man. The bride was attired in a gown of white Duchesse satin, and wore a small wreath of orange blossoms under her tulle veil, her only ornament being a pearl necklace and pendant (the gift of the bridegroom), and her lovely shower bouquet being composed exclusively of choice white flowers. The bridesmaids were all dressed alike in pink and white striped silk skirts, with bodices of Valencienne lace and muslin over pink, and large black velvet hats. They wore gold bangles, and carried shower bouquets of pink carnations, both being gifts of the bridegroom.

After the ceremony—to the strains of the organ and the merry pealing of the bells—the bridal party drove to the residence of a mutual friend in Cromwell Road, where the happy couple were "At home" to a numerous assemblage of relatives and friends, the invited guests from Tonbridge including Mr. and Mrs. J. W. Little, Mr. and Mrs. E. C. Goldberg, Mr. R. H. Bartram, Mrs. G. W. Bartram, Mr. H. B. Nicholl and Miss Wood, and others. Later on—amidst showers of rice and torrents of benediction—Mr. and Mrs. Rogerson departed from their friends, to commence together the journey of life amongst the wild picturesqueness of Snowdonia and the North Wales coast.

The bride wore as a travelling dress a black and white silk gown with dark rose-coloured chéné silk bodice trimmed with lace, and black velvet hat

Newspaper clipping: TONBRIDGE marriage of Mr J. W. Rogerson

When I last heard from these cousins, Michael Rogerson was running his own marketing company in Henley and he, his wife Sheila Hyndman and their two daughters, Catherine and Louise, were living in Hampshire. His younger brother, Major

John Rogerson was living in Canterbury having previously served in Aden, Hongkong and Germany with the Queen's Regiment (formerly East Surrey & Queen's Royal). He met his Irish wife, Olive Stewart, when she was working as a nurse out in Germany. They were married in 1965 and have three children: Simon (born 1967), Sarah (born 1969) and Phillip (born 1973). The middle brother, Timothy Rogerson, emigrated to New Zealand in 1966 having spent thirteen years in the British army. When last heard of he was a colonel in the New Zealand territorial army and a director of the Prudential Insurance company in Wellington, with two daughters, Emma (born 1962) and Philippa (born 1966).

Charles Thomas Rogerson, 'Uncle Charlie', was born 1 July 1865. Charles ran Edward Wells, an old brewery business that had been founded in 1720. It was one of the two breweries in Wallingford, a market town perched on the borders of Oxfordshire and Berkshire, with a handsome corn exchange, the ruins of a medieval priory and a castle, sixty pubs and seventeen maltings. In 1896 Edward Wells was reorganised as the Wallingford Brewery Co Ltd and valued at £150,000 when it possessed eighty-two tied public houses as well as a soft drinks and mineral water bottling plant. In the 1911 census Charles Thomas Rogerson is listed as managing director of the Wallingford Brewery Co. Ltd, aged 45. The brewery would ultimately be taken over in 1928 by the Wiltshire brewery of Ushers. Charles's wife Florence was the youngest of five sisters who had been brought up at St Mary's Priory. She and her husband looked after her father (Thomas Dodd) in his own house in his old age, and afterwards took on the house.

They had two daughters, Florence Miriam Rogerson and Gladys Rogerson. In Tunisia I met one of their old neighbours. She remembered Charles Rogerson as a kind and hospitable man, who occupied a large, comfortable house that was forever filled with the cousins and friends of his two daughters, Gladys and Miriam. She recalled wonderful long tennis parties in the summer attended by players from Wimbledon and remembered a particularly keen match when their dashing cousin, John Rogerson, managed to beat a champion. In the First World War both she and Miriam Rogerson had become volunteer nurses. Miriam Rogerson

Newspaper clipping: Marriage of Mr C.T.Rogerson and Miss F.M.Dodd

fell in love with one of her patients, Gilbert Spence, whom she later married. Her friend remembered that Gilbert was one of four brothers in uniform and his family came from Scotland via South Africa.

Charles Thomas Rogerson died on 9th December 1937. Gladys Rogerson had married J.P. Wallingford and they remained in occupation of the old home from where she would serve for years as the local J.P. She was known to be tough on driving offences, for after her experiences in the First World War, she had decided never to drive again. After her death the family possessions must have been dispersed. A dealer noticed the inscription on the gold watch and got in touch with the nearest Rogerson, which turned out to be me. It was given to Charles on his twenty first birthday by his loving parents, and made just around the corner from where I live in London.

Minnie Ada Rogerson was born in 1863 and lived with her parents all her life. She was known as 'mad Aunt Minnie.'

The Revd Sidney Rogerson was born 23 August 1867. He is easy to identify from the Victorian family photograph with his dog collar and a thoughtful, inquiring face. He was also a bit of a star on the football pitch. He graduated from Cambridge university and would live all over England, working as a parish priest. From 1894-6 he was curate at St Nicholas Winterbourne in Dorset, then spent a long time in the diocese of Yorkshire before returning 'home' to Suffolk and moving to Cambridge in retirement where he died in 1957, aged ninety. He was always much in demand for family ceremonies though he could prove to be a bit of a double-edged weapon. Sidney, like many of his family, was a bit deaf but he retained a clear voice and a keen interest in his surroundings. His critical summaries, delivered as he climbed the steps up to the pulpit, in what he believed to be *sotto voce*, could be dreadfully wounding to the individuals in the congregation. He had his own deep wound, locked up in his passionate devotion to his first young wife, Mary Carroll. Mary was the daughter of Rev Thomas Carroll (1841-1912), vicar of Whitton in Middlesex, the son of John Thomas Carroll (1817-45) from Carollina in County Cork. After their marriage they produced a number of healthy children but they were warned by a doctor that Mary's health might be threatened if she had another child. After giving birth to her fifth child Mary became seriously ill. Despite the most loving and attentive care at their home in Pateley Bridge, she wandered off one afternoon and was later found drowned. The grieving widower turned his housekeeper Sarah Toovey into a loving stepmother with his second marriage.

THE REV. SIDNEY ROGERSON.—The following extract from the *Middlesex Chronicle* will prove interesting to many of our readers, as the gentleman to whom it refers is the son of our respected townsman, Mr. J. W. S. Rogerson, and most of the people in Hoddesdon, who have known him from his youth, have watched his career with interest :—"The Rev. S. Rogerson, the curate of St. Stephen's, will vacate his position in August next, having been appointed to the curacy of Bere Regis, Dorsetshire. During the three years the rev. gentleman has resided here, he has not only gained golden opinions among the members of the congregation of St. Stephen's for the zeal he has displayed in the discharge of his duties, but his amiable disposition, combined with a genial temperament, has made him a real social favourite. Among the young men of the district especially, with whose welfare both spiritually and socially he has closely identified himself, he has come to be regarded with something like brotherly affection, and the announcement of his resignation has been received with general regret by all who have known him." Referring to this subject in the current number of *St. Stephen's Magazine* the Rev. H. Layton, M.A., writes : " He (the Rev. S. Rogerson) came to us at Christmas, 1890, and so has remained longer than is usual in a first curacy. We shall all deeply regret his departure, for he has proved himself an earnest and untiring worker, loyal to his Vicar, and a faithful and true friend to all. We cordially wish him God's blessing, and much happiness in his new parish, which will be in very many respects greatly different from this ; but it will be God's work in the Church all the same, and we are sure that our good friend will work as zealously there as here." The Rev. S. Rogerson is well known in football circles, as for several years he was a prominent member of the Hoddesdon team while they were holders of the cup.

Newspaper clipping: The Rev Sidney Rogerson

(Colonel) Sidney Rogerson (born 22 October 1894, died 1968) was the eldest child of the Revd Sidney Rogerson. His earliest childhood memories were of a long, low and thatched cottage in the heart of Dorset, followed by a vicarage amidst the mill chimneys of Bradford, succeeded by one in the Yorkshire Dales. Sidney was educated at Worksop College from where he went to Cambridge to read History at Sidney Sussex College. Having received his degree in 1916 he served in the West Yorkshire Regiment from 1916-19. He would write a memoir of his experiences as a young officer in the 1916 battle of the Somme, *Twelve Days*, as well as a historical account of the Battle of Aisne, *The Last of the Ebb*. From 1923–30 he organised publicity for the Federation of British Industries, before moving to ICI in 1930. In 1938 his book, *Propaganda in the Next War*, was published. It is a fascinating account of the success of the British propaganda

THE MARRIAGE OF THE REV. S.
ROGERSON AND MISS CARROLL.

On Wednesday, at the church of SS. Philip and
James, Whitton, the Rev. Sydney Rogerson,
former curate of St. Stephen's Church, was united
in matrimony to Miss Mary Carroll, daughter of
the Rev. T. Carroll, vicar of Whitton. The
church was crowded, a great number of those
present being parishioners of St. Stephen's, with
whom Mr. Rogerson had been a great favourite.
The Rev. T. Carroll, assisted by the Rev. J.
Carroll, uncle of the bride, officiated at the
ceremony. The bride looked exceedingly well in a
trained cream cashmere gown, the bodice being
extensively trimmed with cream silk lace and
orange blossoms, whilst a spray of the same
appropriate flower fastened her veil to
her hair. Her bouquet was of white
exotics and orange blossom, intermingled
with asparagus and other fern. The bridesmaids were Miss Ivy Carroll, sister to the
bride, and Miss Lucy Rogerson, sister to the
bridegroom, and both looked handsome in stylish
dresses of salmon-pink cashmere, finished off with
ribbon to match. Their hats were brown straw,
with an edging of jet, and were trimmed with pink
velvet to match, bouquets of yellow roses com-
pleting their costumes. The bridegroom, attended
by his brother, awaited the coming of the bride at
the chancel steps, where the ceremony was
commenced, Mrs. Carroll, mother of the bride,
giving her away. The solemnization over, the
joyful bride and bridegroom left the church amid
congratulations on all sides and showers of rice,
Miss Richards playing "The Wedding March" on
the organ. The Rev. S. and Mrs. Rogerson are
spending their honeymoon at St. Leonard's. The
following is a list of the presents :—

Rev T. Carroll, sewing machine ; Mrs Carroll, salt-
cellars ; Miss Ivy Carroll, centre piece ; Mr J. E. M.
Carroll, afternoon tea table ; Master C. E. Carroll,
thimble ; Master Desmond Carroll, pickle fork ; Mr
and Mrs Rogerson, piano ; Rev A. W. and Mrs
Rogerson, lamp ; Mr J. W. Rogerson, dinner service ;
Mr C. T. Rogerson, table knives ; Mr H. P. Rogerson,
table plate ; Mr F. Rogerson, tumblers, glass, &c. ;
Mr H. Rogerson, decanters ; Miss Rogerson, breakfast
service ; Miss L. Rogerson, tea service ; E. Allum,
shawl ; Dr and Mrs Ball, revolving bookstand ; Mrs
Ball, toilet jar ; E. and J. Ball, fancy baskets ; Mrs
Bartlett, sardine fork ; Mr and Mrs Baughan, brass
coal scuttle ; Mrs Bond, cushion ; Dr and Mrs Brown,
Maltese lace d'oyleys ; Mr G. F. Campion, cheque ; Mr
and Mrs J. H. Carroll, brass kettle and crumb scoop ;
Mr and Mrs T. F. Carroll, cheque ; Mr and Mrs J. T.
Carroll, silver salt-cellars ; Mr and Mrs J. H. Carroll,

Newspaper clipping: Marriage of Mr C. T. Rogerson
and Miss F. M. Dodd

and intelligence campaigns during the First World
War, and our diminishing prospects for pursuing
a similarly successful strategy in any (forthcoming)
conflict. In April 1939 he visited the USA and was
outed as a manipulative British secret agent in an
American media storm. He was no such thing but

was a member of the Travellers Club and knew his
way around Whitehall. He was loaned by ICI for
government service during the Second World War,
and then again to the War Office from 1952-54. He
would also write about the English countryside, *Old
Enchantment*, *Our Bird Book* and *Both Sides of the Road*,
the latter two illustrated by Charles Tunnicliffe.
When not working out of a flat in London (43,
Albert Hall Mansions, Kensington), he lived in
Barningham in Suffolk.

With his first wife, Dorothy, the daughter of
Sir Harry Gibson, Sidney Rogerson had just one
child, Jeremy. Family history tragically repeated
itself. Dorothy became depressed after giving birth
and would be confined to a hospital for most of
her life. Sidney took a second wife, Nancy Allport
with whom he had a daughter Jane and a second
son Peter (born 1940). Jane Rogerson moved to
Australia with her husband Patrick Williams, who
worked for AMP in Sydney. They had two children,
Hugh and Caroline. Peter Rogerson served in the
army then was employed within B.P. He married
Rose Hunt and they had three children, Sarah
Rogerson, James Rogerson and Thomas Rogerson.

Sarah Rogerson married Rupert Reed in 2007
and they have two children, Willoughby (born in
2010) and Grace (born in in 2014). Tom Rogerson
married Tassa Paris and they have one son Benjamin
Rogerson (born 2018) and all live near Woodbridge,
Suffolk so continuing the long Rogerson family
connection with East Anglia.

Jeremy Rogerson joined the Royal Navy and
commanded three ships but decided to leave with
the rank of Commander. He went out into the
world to make enough to bring up a family. He
became a senior partner with the stockbroking firm
of Sheppard & Chase and lived with his wife Tessa
Crimmin in a lovely old farmhouse in the village
of Dedham, on the Essex border with Suffolk. He
dug up all sorts of family press clippings on my last
visit. He has a portrait of his grandfather (one of
the Revd Sidney) and one of his father (Colonel
Sidney) hanging in his dining room in Essex. I
was admiring their thoughtful faces, but as I did
so, Jeremy modestly explained that the confident
public persona of his father had only been achieved
through the most determined effort. His father
battled against depression all his life and could be
consumed by anxiety as one might expect from a

Children surrounding Sidney Rogerson

young man who had experienced two years of trench warfare in addition to the tragic early death of his mother and the insanity of his first wife. He also felt embittered that the animosity of a senior civil servant had undermined the end of his professional career at the War Office.

Jeremy and Tessa had three children: Philippa Jane Rogerson (born 24 April 1961), Mark Christopher Rogerson (born 9 September 1962) and John Russell Rogerson (born 1966). Mark Rogerson worked in The City and his brother John Rogerson is immersed in computer things. John Rogerson married Annabel Fletcher Christian and they have a son Max Jago Rogerson (born 26 September 2011) and a daughter India Chloe Christian Rogerson (born 23 June 2016). Philipa Rogerson, MA, PhD, is known as 'Pippa' and teaches law at Cambridge University, concentrating on the law of international commercial disputes. She is currently the 43rd Master of Gonville & Caius College (the first woman to be elected) and mother of five pony-loving Fitzsimon daughters, Olivia (born 1991), Harriet (born 1993), Beatrice (born 1995), Izzy (born 1997) and Amelia (born

2004). Their father, Gerry Fitzsimmons died too young, in 2007.

Phyllis Rogerson looked after her father, the Revd Sidney Rogerson in his old age. She later married an Anglican clergyman (the Revd Streatfield) and lived in Cambridge. Ursula Rogerson was Phyllis's older sister. She married Patrick Homan and had two children, Rosemary (who married Graham Cooper and produced three children) and Duncan, who married Jill and had two children.

The fifth child of Mary and Sidney Rogerson was born in Yorkshire in 1912 and baptised William Thomas Carroll Rogerson. He was known as 'Bill' and was charming, handsome and headstrong. He married Barbara Lees at Hepworth, Suffolk in the autumn of 1935. Barbara was born in Cassington, Essex and was the daughter of a vicar. Two years later she gave birth to a son, Anthony Carroll Rogerson. By the end of the Second World War Bill had risen to the rank of Lieutenant-Colonel but instead of allowing himself to be disbanded and packed off back to England he decided to stay on in Italy and started trading in the free-wheeling post-war marketplace. In 1946 he divorced his English

Bill, Major William Rogerson

Bill and Andrea Rogerson

wife and in 1948 married his Italian girlfriend Marissa Belvieglieri, with whom he had a second son, Andrew. I remember my grandfather recalling a week of shooting with him in the 60's based in a decaying but magnificent castle that Bill rented. On another occasion he came back to visit his family in Suffolk, driving a car 'bigger than the village" according to my grandfather. Later on he shed the aura of a merchant-adventurer and set up Mercantile Italo-Britannia with its head office in Rome. They represented thirty British aerospace companies, specialising in radar, electronics and Rolls-Royce jet engines and both managed their importation and licencing agreements with allied Italian industrialists. Bill received the CBE for service to British industry in 1975 and died in Orvieto in 1983. His widow Marissa later remarried Count Giancarlo Ferreti, and they died in 2006 and 2013.

Bill's eldest son Anthony Rogerson went to Oxford University, spent 16 years in the RAF as an education officer, then 14 years with a Christian missionary society, then set up a management training company in Oxford before finally taking up holy orders. The Revd Anthony Rogerson lives in Radley, Oxford and with his wife Heather Graham. They have three children, Tom Rogerson (born 1961), Paul Rogerson (born in 1963) and Hugh Rogerson (born in 1966).

Tom Rogerson (born 1961) is married to Hilary, they have two sons, Luke and Patrick (born 1990).

Paul Rogerson (born in 1963) was married to Mara. They have two sons, Daniel and Patrick.

Andrea (Andrew Philip Rogerson) was born in Italy in 1950. He is Bill's second son, who much later in life would also be adopted by his Italian stepfather. He was educated at Eton, then Cambridge University and the LSE. He would become an economist, serving as a Director of the World Bank then a senior civil servant and a consultant advising on Aid to developing countries. He and his wife (Carole Finney) live in London and have two sons, Mathew and John.

Mathew William Rogerson (born 19 November 1981) married Ling Ling Phung.

John Patrick Rogerson (born 4 March 1983) is married to Natasha Barrero with a son, William Rogerson (born 2 December 2012) and a daughter Beatrice Rogerson (born 2015.)

Herbert Peter Rogerson (1869–1925) married Florence Scruby in 1896 who had been born in Harlow, Essex. They lived in the Hertfordshire town of Bishops Stortford, in a house on Havers Lane. Herbert ran a malting house and they had three children: Gerald Rogerson (born 1900), Ronald K.V. Rogerson (born 1904) and Anthea Rose Rogerson (born 1907). Ronald married Margaret Lawrie in 1937 and died 1967.

Frank Rogerson was born in 1872, the seventh child of Lucy and Josiah. He married Florence Emily Allenby, daughter of Louis Charles Allenby on 25 April 1896 at St Luke's, Lambeth. They had five children: Evelyn, Hugh, John, Michael and Betty.

Evelyn Victoria Rogerson (Aunt Eve) married William R.S. Smith, no children.

Hugh Stanley Rogerson married Gertrude Rochford in 1925, daughter of Thomas Rochford of Turners Hall, Hertfordshire. They had two sons, Barry Hugh Rogerson and Keith Frank Rogerson. After the death of his first wife Hugh married Olivia Worthington and had a son, Nico Rogerson. Nico would have three wives; Elizabeth Rummel, Caroline Le Bas and Dinah Nicolson. Nico was a much loved step-father (to Michael and Sandy Rummel-Grock) from his first marriage and to Dicken Verry and Georgia Fiennes from his third marriage, but has no blood descendants.

Barry married Peggy Page-Croft (first wife of Richard Page-Croft with whom she had three children; Hugo, Miriam and Ricky) and they had a daughter Emma Rogerson with Barry. After Peggy's death, Barry married Heather, a widow.

Keith Frank Rogerson (born 26 October 1928 and died 8 July 2004) married Kathleen Moira Harvie (born 4 February 1927 and died 6 May 2014). Kathy was the third child of Major J.K.Harvie (3rd Hussars) and Mary Bushby Stubbs, M.M, and Croix de Guerre. They had four children: Diana Mary Rogerson (Dido), David Keith Rogerson, Barnaby Hugh Rogerson and James Francis Rogerson.

Dido's first child, Katherine Louise Ashling (Roo), was with Christopher Wallis, after which she had four children with the musician Stephen Stapleton: Lilith (Lili), Louis, Luke Lawless and Django. Roo lives in Ireland and teaches Art (especially photography) at the university of Galway. She had a son Freddie Burrows (who is a circus acrobat) with a handsome young musician called Peat and half a generation later a second child (Rowan) with her husband Gerald Glynn. Lili is another of the horse-people in our family and has a daughter, Isobel (Issy) who seems to be going the same way. Louis, Luke and Django also live in the Burren hills of County Clare during covid lockdowns but otherwise are found working their way around the globe.

David lives in Venezuela with his wife Ysbelia Briceno and his stepson Wilfredo.

Barnaby Rogerson is married to Rose Baring who works as a psychoanalytical psychotherapist. Rose's mother, born Susan Mary Renwick 5 June 1930 worked as a J.P. in Hampshire and become fascinated by the work of the probation service and international human rights and stood as a liberal parliamentary candidate. Rose and Barnaby run a publishing company together, called Eland which reprints classic travel books.

They have two daughters: Molly Francis Tripoli Rogerson was born 8 June 1995. She works as a Veterinary Nurse in the R.V.C London training hospital. Hannah Ruby Primrose Rogerson was born 21 February 1998. She is studying Anthropology at Edinburgh University.

James Rogerson married Corinna Stahl. They live in Switzerland and have two children, Carlotta and Nicholas.

Carlotta is an apprentice trainer in Germany and has just been selected to be in the Swiss national dressage team. Nicholas is studying online business at Barcelona university and playing a lot of polo.

John (Frank Leslie) Rogerson was born 31 July 1902. He married Eileen Daphne Solvia Joel, who was born 20 March 1907 and died 30 January 1974. They had one daughter, Valda Rogerson. Valda's first husband was Timothy Nicolson from a family long involved in India, with a shipping business and tea plantations in Assam, amongst other enterprises. They had two children together, Euan Nicolson and Alastair Nicolson. Valda's second marriage was to Nicholas Embiricos (from a family of Greek ship-owners) with whom she had a daughter, Alexandra Embiricos, who is a horsewoman like her mother and grandmother before her.

Euan works in the City (energy insurance) in one of those gleaming skyscrapers beside the Lloyds

Building. He is married to Emma Carr-Smiley. They have a son, called Hector.

Alastair John Nicolson (born 24 Nov 1959) trained as an architect and has brought up three children with his Dutch wife, Juliette Bogaers (who trained as an art historian and worked as an antique dealer) but is now involved in a charity helping old Dutch people.

Iona Nicolson (born 19 September 1995) is about to start working as a lawyer; Adair Nicolson (born 25 June 1998) has completed his MSc Natural Sciences (Chemistry/Physics) and will go to UCL on perovskite solar panel research; Isla Nicolson (born 4 August 2001) is about to go to Imperial College to study Geology.

Michael Dennis Rogerson (born 26 July 1910) married Marion Hilda Brownrigg (born 30 July 1914) in 1939. They had three children; Mark Annesley Rogerson (born 29 April 1942), Mary Louise Rogerson (born 1 August 1945) and Matthew Frank Rogerson (born 4 October 1950). Marion died aged ninety in 2004. She was educated in Battle Abbey (built on the hill where King Harold was killed by the Norman invaders). As head-girl she safely evacuated the entire school from a fire and rescued the property deeds. She was working as window dresser for Jaeger when she fell in love with Michael having met at a dance in Haslemere. Marion's brother Charles Brownrigg took on the headmastership of Fernden. Marion had two sisters. Sheila married Wing-Cdr Dudley Farmer (who bombed Cottesmore with sweets) and Pansy married Sir Ronald Prain, who made a fortune from copper mines, working hand in glove with the independent states emerging in Africa.

Mark (the second Rogerson headmaster of Cottesmore) married Cathryn Ann Daly (born 7 October 1942) and they had four children; Annabel Colette Rogerson (29 September 1965), Samuel Peter Annesley Rogerson (14 June 1970), Lucy Elizabeth Rogerson (5 September 1971) and Thomas Frank Rogerson (30 May 1975).

Annabelle has four children (Polly, Frank, Louisa and Isabel) with Tim Wates, the working family director within the Wates Group.

Samuel Rogerson used to work as a Television Producer but has reverted to the family fascination with education, albeit outside traditional forms.

He married his boss Sophie Oliver and has two children: Noah (born 25 April 2003) and Kitty (born 5 August 2005). They live in Haslemere.

Lucy is a physiotherapist and has three children with her husband Benedict Knollys who is a wine merchant (Hatch Mansfield): Frederick William (born 2006), Jessamy Eva Ellen (born 2008) and Sienna Cathryn (born 2011).

Thomas Rogerson (who is the third headmaster of Cottesmore) married Charlotte Curtis and has two children, Wilfred (born 31 December 2012) and Edward Mark, known as 'Bear'.

Mary-Lou Rogerson was born 1 August 1945 and married Francis Hussey in April 1970. Mary-Lou went to Southover School in Lewes, Sussex topped up by a finishing school in Switzerland to improve her French. Like Aunt Eve before her, she set up her own dress shop, called Sheba. Mary Lou inherited her mothers kindness and sense of calm, which disappeared the moment you played 'racing demon' for her nails were painted by blood red for a good reason. Mary-Lou and Francis had two daughters Letitia (Sophie) born on 12 April 1972 and Antonia Natasha (Sasha) born 4 January 1974. Francis Hussey was born 21 January 1941, the son of Dyneley Hussey, music critic, war- poet and author of biographies of Mozart and Verdi. Francis was educated at King's, Canterbury, then went up to Corpus Christi College, Oxford to read PPE. He taught history and politics A level for 20 years (St George's Weybridge 1966-75, Belmont Abbey, Herefordshire 1975-87) and then 13 years in the wine trade. Mary-Lou Rogerson taught herself to be an artist whilst bringing up their two daughters.

Sophie is currently head of development at the Royal Central School of Speech and Drama, having previously worked at the Royal Opera House, Royal Court Theatre and Royal College of Music. She is married to Alan Bain, head of the drawing office at the National Theatre, and they have two daughters: Elodie Marion Bain (born 29 September 2005) and Clara Irene Bain (born 27 August 2008). Sasha married Seth Forsyth and they have a son, Zachariah Gale Forsyth born 29 March 2008. Matthew Rogerson (born 4 October 1950) ran the Cottesmore Hotel, Golf & Country Club which he set up with his father, successfully growing the business into a twenty-six room hotel, with seven self-catering lodges, a nineteen hole golf course, a spa and an eight hole course with the ability to manage conferences and weddings. When Nanty died in 1977 she left Mathew enough money in her will for him to build his own house, which was named Challis Wood in her honour. Mathew married his 'island girl' Susan Gaynor Cheeseman on 31 July 1976. Susan was born on the Isle of Wight, specialised in teaching dyslexia and enjoyed listening to her own father (who was a Quaker and the headmaster of a Comprehensive School) discussing educational issues with her father-in-law. Mathew and Susan have three children; Helen Elizabeth Rogerson (born 9 May 1978), John Benjamin Rogerson (3 May 1980) and Louisa Marian Rogerson (born 30 August 1983).

Helen has two sons (Max and Luke) with her partner Charlie Karabou.

Louisa and her husband Johnnie Porter have three sons (Toby, Charlie and William). They worked with Mathew and took over the running of the Club in the summer of 2013.

John Rogerson (an artist and a teacher) and his new wife Zeema have just had a daughter, Cordelia.

Betty Rogerson married Patrick Milligan and had two children, Richard Milligan and Jennifer Milligan.

Richard Milligan worked in Lloyds Insurance and married Angela and had two children Jemma Milligan and Joshua Milligan.

Jennifer Milligan married Richard Wills, who also worked in Lloyds Insurance. They had three children: Simon Richard Wills (born 20 August 1960), Sophia Mary Wills (born 2nd September 1962) and Patrick Grant Wills (born 22 May 1965).

Sophie married Robert Newton and they had Matthew David Newton (born 15 November 1984), Anna Georgina Newton (24 January 1986) and Olivia Mary Newton (4 August 1989) together before they got divorced. All three of her children are now married. Georgina married Daniel Comer and has two children of her own, Dahlia and Birdie.

Simon Wills married Amanda Freeman and had Samuel Richard (29 March 1993) and Sasha Rosalind (28 November 1995) before they separated.

Patrick Wills married Denise Hribal and they had two children, Ella Nicola (6 March 1997) and Anna Mary (14 May 1999) before they divorced.

Harry Finch Rogerson was the eighth child of Lucy and Josiah, born 28 March 1874. When his father left the brewery, Harry and Lucy moved with him to Lindon Lodge, Alcester road, Surrey. Harry ran a Brewery in Wokingham, Berkshire and in due course married Madge Collingwood, the daughter of a Naval officer.

Their son Cuthbert Harry Rogerson, MB BS Lond(1932), MD Lond(1933), DPM Eng(1936), MRCS LRCP(1931), MRCP(1934,) FRCP(1945), had the most exceptional mind of all his cousins. Cuthbert was born in Wokingham on 25 April 1909 and died 10 February 1949 aged forty.

Although never robust after the removal of a kidney, he was an outstanding student at Haileybury College and at Guy's Hospital, and in 1934 went on a Rockefeller scholarship to the Phipps Clinic of the Johns Hopkins Hospital in Baltimore. This experience had a permanent influence, for in 1937 he returned to Guy's Hospital to study psychiatric problems in children as Sir Alfred Fripp fellow, and set up an active unit which attracted both post-graduates and social workers. That year he also became medical director of the Cassel Hospital for Functional Nervous Disorders at Swaylands, Kent, and psychotherapist to the Hill End Hospital, St. Albans, remarkable achievements for a young man of twenty-eight, who was able to cope successfully with the difficulties involved in the move to the Midlands on the outbreak of war in 1939. At the end of war, in 1946 he accepted the invitation to become director of the Seton Institute in Baltimore, Maryland, and set about changing an old fashioned mental hospital into an up-to-date curative one. He also established himself as an outstanding teacher and had been appointed lecturer to the Catholic University, Washington DC when he developed a brain tumour and died in 1949 at the age of forty. Rogerson's infinite thirst for knowledge, his phenomenal memory and his facility of expression were shown in his conversation, his lectures, and the many contributions he made to medical journals. His interests were wide: botany, art, Greek, medieval poetry and mathematics. He was a good listener, and therefore able to effect change by quiet suggestion.

In 1936 Cuthbert married Betty Freeman, a vivacious American girl who was a fine athlete but chiefly involved in her own academic work in the field of statistics. Her father was Allen C. Freeman, a professor of public health administration at John Hopkins University. They had two sons (one called Michael Rogerson) who lived in America. By chance when we lived in Virginia, we discovered that our next-door neighbour (Annie Adler) was a cousin of Betty. Annie's father had written a pair of monumental biographies on George Washington and Robert E Lee.

Lucy Rogerson, the youngest of the family of Josiah Rogerson was born 18 July 1877. She married Rock and give birth to two children: Rosemary and James, who was known as Jim.

APPENDIX TWO

Who is Sidney Rogerson?

Better to write for yourself and have no public, than to write for the public and have no self.
Cyril Connolly

A Bear Coughs: A Cautionary Tale of Propaganda

An article written by Sidney Rogerson for the *New Yorker* in June 1957

The announcement of the forthcoming visit of Queen Elizabeth II to the United States recalls to my memory a singular experience which befell me at the time of the visit of her father and mother to America in 1939. I was on my first visit to the United States and it impressed on me the truth that 'Luck' is the one indispensable to success in 'Life'.

My experience taught me – as you shall hear – how a man's career can even be affected by the action of an unknown being on the other side of the world. There is a saying 'A bear coughs at the North Pole and a man dies in Peking.' In my case an enthusiastic isolationist acted on an impulse and I nearly lost my job in London, England.

It all happened in the spring of 1939 when the nerves of the world were jangling and over-taut under the threat of the Second World War. The shadows of the European dictators fell over the lives of the ordinary people of the New World as well as of the Old and provided ample excuse for frayed tempers and over-active suspicions.

The year before I had written a book, a volume in a 'Next War' series edited by my friend Basil Liddell Hart, the well-known military expert, designed to give the British public a picture of the sort of situation that they could expect to see develop at sea, in the air and on land if the threatened struggle came to pass. My volume was *Propaganda in the Next War* and in it, after noting how propaganda, or political warfare as it is now called, had proved itself so potent an engine of

war during the war of 1914-18, I outlined how the British could both use it and defend themselves against its use in the coming upheaval. It was an almost astringently objective study, openly casting Germany, Italy and Japan as the villains of the piece and discussing their strengths and weaknesses in a war of words and ideas. Naturally I referred also the undeclared neutrals, among whom the greatest was the United States. Indeed, I identified her as 'the Great Neutral', who would not be likely to enter a war unless she was almost compelled to do so. So I wrote:

> Great Britain will need too much propaganda to keep the United States benevolently neutral. To persuade her to take our part will be much more difficult, so difficult as to be unlikely to succeed. It will need a definite threat to America, a threat, moreover, which will have to be brought home by propaganda to every citizen, before the republic will again take arms in an external quarrel. The position will naturally be considerably eased if Japan were involved and this might and probably would bring America in without further ado. At any rate, it would be a natural and obvious object of our propagandists to achieve this, just as during the Great War they succeeded in embroiling the United States with Germany.

This was no more than an underlining of the obvious, and that the United States was eventually embroiled was happily not down to the wiles of Britain's word warfare, but to grievous miscalculation of the Japanese. Nevertheless, the passage and indeed my

Colonel Sidney Rogerson

whole section on 'Enemies, Neutrals and Allies', literally raised the roof in the United States and rocked my prospects of my career in England.

Propaganda had appeared in Great Britain in 1938. It was extensively reviewed, but in the United States it got less attention than I had hoped for, and although review copies were sent to all the larger and more responsible American papers, only two or three notices could be traced.

In April 1939 I was sent to The United States to visit and report on the New York World's Fair. Here is where the bear coughed! I landed on 25 April and about a week later I woke to find myself posed most embarrassingly in the limelight of US national affairs. Throughout the country, papers of all types, weighty and flighty, had either led their news with or had prominently featured a story that Great Britain was attempting to trick the US into any war that might be coming. In evidence of this sinister plot they cited *Propaganda in the Next War* and asked indignantly but understandably, 'Who is Sidney Rogerson?' The story was inspired by the fact that on the day I had set foot in America Senator Nye of Indiana, an impassioned isolationist, had referred

in the Senate to *Propaganda*, and had even had the offending chapter on 'Neutrals' read into the Congressional Record where it may be seen to this day. He sought to make his hearers' flesh creep by telling them how he had been allowed to see a copy of the book which was, he declared, a textbook for the political warfare experts of Great Britain, and was the only copy which had found its way into the United States – a leakage which, he asserted, had so alarmed the British authorities that they had promptly suppressed the book. Such wild talk was not only nonsense but wholly untrue as more than one Senator and some of the more reliable newspapers bluntly told Senator Nye. They even told him who Sidney Rogerson was! For example, the *Springfield Republican* (Mass.) on 12th May informed its readers *Propaganda* was as accessible (in the United States) as 'Gone with the Wind' and further accused those who put about printed statements to the contrary of being guilty of 'gross dishonesty or gross journalistic fault'. Not so the *New Yorker*, which mentioned the incident in 'Talk of the Town' and ended their references with the statement that 'We are rather sorry that the British authorities have decided to suppress Mr Rogerson's book. We had a place waiting for it on our bookshelf, right beside *Mein Kampf*', which all goes to show that even the most cynical, worldly-wise of magazines can fall as heavily as the small-town-news rag. The rumpus was obviously engineered by the isolationist camp to influence public opinion against any abandonment by the United States of what was still her non-interventionist tradition.

The first of this was that I was the subject of the very thing about which *Propaganda* was written – the twists and perversions of the truth which are employed by nations and governments to influence their people and their enemies in times of war or crisis. *The New York Telegram* actually urged its readers, 'If you want peace, write to Congress', exactly as the Communists and fellow-travellers today try to hold up Western defence by getting up public agitation for peace. I was literally 'hoisted by my own petard'. This unwanted and indeed inexplicable continent-wide publicity made me most unpopular with my hosts, Messrs Dupont de Nemours. Then as now they were being smelt out by the witch-doctors of the Anti-Trust office and the inquisitors of the Sherman Act. To have it known that they were giving hospitality to me who was being built up as a subversive alien would have been most embarrassing, to say the least. They begged me to go 'to ground' and here is the second moral of this extraordinary incident. Although there were twenty or thirty newspapermen, friends of mine, who knew full well that I was in New York, not one of these, in answer to my plea, disclosed my presence, much less tried to exploit it – a noteworthy example of the honour and trust which characterises the journalistic profession. Meanwhile, I was content to laugh the things off, and even to preen myself in the glare of such publicity, though two thoughts continued to puzzle me as to why the bear had coughed when and how it did.

The first was why had a space of months elapsed between the US papers receiving review copies of *Propaganda* in September 1938, and Senator Nye raising the issue in the Senate in April 1939. My only explanation was that he had timed his attack in order to prejudice the success of the state visit of King George VI and Queen Elizabeth, which was to take place later in the month. Again this was the very thing I had treated of in *Propaganda*.

The second question was why did not the nationwide publicity flare up until nearly a week after the Senate debate? So concerted a blaze could not, I argued, have broken out unless someone had deliberately organised it by pouring gasoline on the embers of the fire left by the Senate debate. The answer to this was not forthcoming until years later when it was explained to me that Senator Nye's effort had not aroused the publicity that he had hoped and so recourse had to be made to other methods to secure the desired result. A hint of what had happened was given in the *New York Word Telegram* on 12 May, which contained the account that Thomas L Stokes, Pullitzer prize winner, was instrumental in getting the news out. He had taken copies of the book to Washington and 'placed them in good hands'. Years later I was told that this was an understatement. He, or someone associated with him, had made copies of the offending section of the book and had circulated them to practically every newspaper of standing in the United States.

In less than a fortnight, the opening of the World's Fair had stolen the headlines, and the press laid off the hunt to welcome the British King and Queen. Only the indefatigable jackals of the Hearst press had the energy to return to the attack again in August 1939 when the Japanese–US Commercial Treaty was abrogated, and Mr Hearst saw in this the influence of what I had written in the offending chapter of *Propaganda*.

Meanwhile, within three weeks after the event, I was back in England with only an amused memory of my first trip to the United States. Had my experience been normal in that astonishing country, I mused, or was I the victim of an unusual set of circumstances? A few days after my return the storm blew up. My chairman, Lord McGowan, sent for me and told me he had had a complaint about my conduct from Lord Tweedsmuir, then Governor General of Canada. The sense of this complaint might be roughly stated as 'How dare I go over to America and engineer such publicity in order to sell my beastly book just before the visit of Their Majesties?' 'The Governor-General tells me' Lord McGowan continued, 'that such publicity is likely to have an adverse effect on US opinion at a critical time'. Such a reading of the incident had never once occurred to me, but as soon as I was accused, I saw how natural it would be for outsiders to argue that my behaviour was no more than to be expected of a young man engaged in public relations who saw in his trip to the United States a priceless opportunity to boost his own work, irrespective of other considerations. Luckily, I had friends who knew me better, and who were able to restrain my chairman from giving me what one of them described as the 'bum's rush'. Instead, my offence was fairly investigated by a panel of the Board of Directors. I was then able not only to answer the charges levelled against me but to turn the tables on my accusers. First, I pointed to the obvious flaws in argument. I had written the book months before. Senator Nye had read it into the Congressional Record before I landed in New York, before I had disembarked – how then could I have engineered such publicity? Next I explained that I had been fully alive to the possible complications arising out of a book like *Propaganda* and in writing it had sought guidance from those who had had official positions in the political-warfare set-up of World War I. Chief among these was the US-educated Canadian, Sir Campbell Stuart, who in 1939 was again occupying an unofficial advisory position to the government on the matter of propaganda. I had consulted him at every step of my manuscript before I had passed it for printing. In other words, *Propaganda* had actually received the off-the-record approval of the Foreign Office.

There remained Lord Tweedsmuir himself whom I had for years known personally as John Buchan and from whom as a young writer I had received much kindness and advice. His complaint I was able to turn neatly against him by producing letters which showed that I had submitted the offending chapter of the book to him for advice, and that he had returned it without correction or adverse comment. I was completely exonerated, but not before I had passed through some anxious moments. What I did not disclose was that my submission of the chapter to Tweedsmuir was dictated not by reasons of State – on which I felt I had covered myself with Campbell Stuart – but because I wanted to impress him, John Buchan, a master of his craft, with the book that I, his admirer, had written – self-advertisement! But lucky that I had done so, and luckier still that I could lay my hands on all the correspondence necessary for my vindication!

APPENDIX THREE

Cottesmore School

Fear not for the future, weep not for the past.
Shelley

Cottesmore School is firmly rooted at Buchan Hill, the magnificent Victorian country house whose ample terraced grounds overlook a succession of lakes and golf courses set against a receding blue-green horizon of wooded hills. Cottesmore School is also firmly linked to the Rogerson family, who for three generations have cherished, taught and watched over a school which is at once their passion, their business and their home. Michael and Marion Rogerson, then Mark and Cathryn Rogerson, and now Thomas and Charlotte Rogerson.

Cottesmore School was founded by Geoffrey Davison-Brown on 3 September 1894. The school opened with just two pupils: Oliver and Standage, but by the end of the term it had nine

and an assistant master. Within a year the house at 50, The Drive, Hove, Sussex was bursting at the seams. A site for a purpose-built boarding school was quickly chosen, an architect briefed and by 20 June 1896 the foundation stone had been laid. In May 1897 it was ready for occupation and over the following decade various sports grounds, a chapel and even a swimming pool were added. Davison-Brown, who was affectionately nicknamed 'the Baron', by both staff and pupils, had a natural gift for teaching, an infectious zest for life and a love of France. His school, which was in competition with literally hundreds of similar establishments on the Sussex coast, thrived in those halcyon years of the early 1900s. Armed with our hindsight of

Architectural proposal sketch by Ernest George and Peto for Buchan Hill House

Cottesmore School in Hove

COTTESMORE SCHOOL

HOVE, BRIGHTON.

Founded in 1894 by the late Major G. Davison Brown, M.A.

Recognised as efficient by the Board of Education.

Preparatory School for Gentlemen's Sons, between the ages of 7 and 14, for the principal Public Schools and the Royal Navy.

THE SCHOOL IS FOR BOARDERS ONLY.

Headmaster :

H. S. FORSTER (Malvern and Magdalen College, Oxford)

— WITH —

F. E. J. MONTAUBAN, M.A. (Charterhouse and Corpus Christi College, Cambridge).

Assisted by four Resident Masters and a Governess.

Cottesmore School Prospectus

events, the foundation of a School Cadet Corps at Cottesmore in the 1890s seems an ironic farce before a looming tragedy. The actual outbreak of war in the autumn of 1914 brought out a subdued (and largely unrecorded) panic in all private schools with fear of air raids, a rash of unpaid bills and absent boys. The cruel devastation of the actual war years is brought home graphically by the stream of obituaries which overwhelmed the Old Cottesmorian magazine. Two whole generations of schoolboys were consumed by the fighting, and many of the survivors were permanently incapacitated. Davison-Brown, who himself served on the front line, never fully recovered from the physical and emotional scars of the war. Mr Baker ran the school during the war but throughout the 1920s Davison -Brown relied on Harry Strong-Forster, his deputy, who formally took over as headmaster on Davison-Brown's death in 1929. Strong-Forster was a taciturn, rather dry character: a dedicated correspondent, a precise classicist and an enthusiastic cricketer. The era over which he presided coincided with the Great Depression which was a testing time for private education (seventy-four of the five hundred preparatory schools closed during the Depression).

In 1936, when Cottesmore was down to just thirty boys, he entered into a partnership with Michael Rogerson who had the necessary experience financial backing and enthusiasm to reverse the school's decline. Michael Rogerson also reinforced the schools numbers by bringing with him seventeen boys from Uplands House. Michael Rogerson's marriage to Marion Brownrigg in 1939 immeasurably strengthened the Cottesmore management. Aside from her own remarkable organisational abilities, she carried with her a sense of dignified, purposeful calm, which was the perfect counterpoise to Michael's questing effervescence. Marion's unshakeable poise was no act. It was bred-in-the bone of the daughter of N. G. Brownrigg, the proprietor-headmaster of Fernden Preparatory School. Norman Graham Brownrigg was one of the seven children of John Annesley Brownrigg who had practiced as a doctor in London. The Brownrigg's were an Anglo-Irish family long based on Norris Mount in County Wexford.

The Second World War tested the Rogerson's mettle to the full. In June 1940 the school

buildings, along with much of the property on the southern coast of England, were requisitioned by the Ministry of Defence, who feared a German invasion. Michael and Marion organised the evacuation of the entire school to the safety of Wales within a few days. They first found lodging at the Oakley Arms Hotel in the vale of Ffestiniog (which Michael had booked a month before with a cash advance), but then two terms later found more permanent and spacious lodging at 17th-century Cors-y-Gedol Hall at Dyffryn. It was a magical place set amongst empty beaches, moorland and mountain streams, and it served as a true sanctuary for the sixty war-time children placed under their care. Just when things had become almost settled Michael Rogerson was called up by the army. His sparse leave was spent at the school, but he was serving as a captain in Normandy when he was informed of the death of Harry Strong-Foster in the autumn of 1944 and was released by the army in order to run the school.

After the war was over he and Marion returned the school briefly to its old home at Hove before acquiring Buchan Hill House and an adjoining farm. Michael had known the place of old, for in the early 1930s he had cut his teeth as a young schoolmaster there, when it housed Upland House Preparatory School. He made certain that the boys would have positive memories of their first day at Buchan Hill House by organising a picnic outing from the old school buildings at Hove. A plane, flown by his brother-in-law, repeatedly buzzed the little group. It made one more turn and then released a cloud of sweets. It was manna from heaven, particularly for children who had grown up in the strict war economy of sugar rationing.

Cottesmore had moved lock stock and barrel from Hove to Buchan Hill House to start the September term, 1946. The traditions and treasured trophies of the old school made the journey too: the old bell, the billiard table, the Barons chair, the Imperial shield, the war-memorial panelling and even the cricket pavilion. New life flooded through the old mansion and its polices. The stable block was converted into staff houses, the old chapel became a gym, a new chapel was made out of the old kitchen and schoolrooms were formed in the old conservatory. In the coming years the vaulted cellars were turned into a shooting gallery and

Approach to Buchan House – when occupied by Uplands School

Back view of Buchan House framed by terrace

Side view of Buchan House

studios for crafts, art and hobbies. One bewildered psychiatrist after a full-day, full-throttle tour of the school under Michael Rogerson's wing murmured 'but when do they have time to dream?' Meanwhile new sportsfields were laid out, a school golf course created and the lake was cleared to make way for swimming, boating and fishing expeditions in the summer and skating in the winter. At the same time, Michael and Marion were attentive parents, kept open house for a positive herd of friends, neighbours, old boys and relations as well as running the home-farm. It was an extraordinarily successful double act that kept Cottesmore as a model of its kind, enthused with a strong dose of individuality and style. They also had the good sense to quit while they were well ahead. In 1971 they handed Cottesmore over to their son Mark and embarked on a world tour. When they returned they moved into a new house built just out of sight of the school. Michael promptly started creating a golf course and country club from the woodland and rough grazing of their farm.

Mark Rogerson was well prepared for the task. Educated at his Brownrigg uncle's prep school,

Fernden, followed by Eton and Churchill College, Cambridge, he went on to practice the craft of teaching at Wellesley House, Broadstairs, followed by Summerfields, Oxford, L'Ecole des Roches in France and then at nearby Windelsham. It was at Windelsham that he met Cathryn Daly, a fellow member of staff. They married in 1969, the year Mark moved over to take up the assistant headmastership at Cottesmore. It was an ideal partnership for Cathryn matched Mark's unflappable confidence and easy charm with her own passionate concern for the happiness of the children. Bit by bit they added their own style and commitment to the life of Cottesmore. Some aspects of traditional boarding-school life, such as nude bathing for learner-swimmers, boxing and corporal punishment were gradually phased out. The heart of their new policy, the creation of a fully co-educational boarding school, was forward thinking. Girl pupils enormously strengthened the familial as opposed to the institutional atmosphere, to improve the whole quality and tone of boarding school life.

A review of schools published in the *Daily Telegraph* provides a survey of Cottesmore: 'Quite exceptional atmosphere: feels like an overgrown family, and a remarkably happy one at that. Staff vigilant and endlessly encouraging; high expectations of behaviour and effort; competition kept in its place, balanced by praise; children obviously happy and secure. Headmaster hugely experienced, very approachable; runs the school shoulder to shoulder with his wife. Believes passionately in the value of boarding. Pupils are open, friendly, busy, delighted to explain what they are doing. Pursuit of excellence combined with compassionate nurturing. Highly recommended.'

Mark and Cathryn Rogerson. Mark has just won the family pewter, a Rogerson family golf match.

Midshipman Rogerson: Life on board HMS Indomitable, the Battle of Jutland and Coaling

You aspire to great things? Begin with little ones.
St Augustine

I joined my first ship, HMS *Indomitable*, with five others of my term, at Rosyth in September 1915. I believe there is a moment at the beginning of every naval officer's career which he remembers vividly. For me, at the age of fifteen, it was like going straight from school into an unknown adult world which I knew would be pretty tough, and I felt apprehensive and rather frightened as I stepped out of the night train at Inverkeithing station. I had received my appointment while on leave at the end of the two months practical training at Keyham, where we had been sent after only two and a half terms at Dartmouth. For some reason our sea chests, instead of being sent straight from the College to our ships, had been sent home and I well remember the consternation among porters and cab drivers in London when asked to handle this huge, heavy article. It would not fit into a taxi and eventually it had to be hoisted on to the roof of a horse-drawn growler which was the only way of getting it across London from Charing Cross to Kings Cross.

We must have been a very comic-looking lot as we came on board, with our youthful faces and squeaky voices. The ship had just finished coaling and I well remember the awe-inspiring figure of our Commander, James Moreton, a very big man, covered from head to foot in coal dust, and the surprised expression on his face as we reported ourselves. He christened us 'The war babies' and immediately ordered an intensive course of capstan drill, which meant jumping down from the capstan with stiff legs to land heavily on our heels. This spine jolting performance was said to be a sure way to make our voices break. Needless to say, it had no effect whatever and we just had to wait for nature to take its course.

Our life as junior midshipmen in the *Indomitable* was hard but by no means as tough as in some other gunrooms at the time. It was traditional that the 'young gentlemen' must be taught that forgetfulness, carelessness and slackness could not be tolerated and that they must develop a proper sense of duty, responsibility and respect for their seniors. Much of this education was done with the aid of the stick, or the threat of the stick, and very effective it proved. I have always been in favour of this sort of punishment for the young provided that it is fairly administered. Do this or forget to do that and the penalty is a dozen or half a dozen over the backside. Fair enough. But, when as sometimes happened, the sub would say, 'All the young gentlemen are getting slack, half a dozen all round,' you did not know exactly what you were being beaten for and it seemed a bit unfair.

Gunroom punishments could only be administered by the sub of the mess, but for some minor offences authority to punish was delegated to the senior midshipman. This was lucky for us because when we joined the sub of the mess was comparatively easy going whereas the other sub and the assistant paymaster were a couple of stinkers and had it been within their power we would have had a very much harder time with many more beatings and very much less justice. As it was, both of them, and the AP in particular, managed to make themselves quite unpleasant enough and delighted to torment us with constant nagging and sarcasm. Later on, another sub took over the mess. If we had hoped for better things,

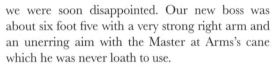

Boxing at Royal Naval College Osborne,
Jerome versus Rogerson, 6 July 1914

Cadet H.S.Rogerson, December 1914

we were soon disappointed. Our new boss was about six foot five with a very strong right arm and an unerring aim with the Master at Arms's cane which he was never loath to use.

A gun room punishment book was kept and during the twelve months or so we did as junior midshipmen the records of beating varied between the six of us. If I remember rightly, I came off best with a mere four dozen while the top score was no less than twelve dozen. This would seem pretty heavy punishment, but I think the young officer in question took it all very much in his stride. Corporal punishment today is said to be sadistic and degrading both to those who administer it and to those on the receiving end. At the time of which I am writing no one had thought up this nonsense and where the young were concerned the use of the cane and the birch was considered the best corrective and its threat a very good deterrent.

Our gunroom contained three commissioned officers. The senior sub-lieutenant, who was Mess President, another sub and a one-stripe assistant paymaster. There were, as well, nine senior

midshipman and an Assistant Clerk who ranked as a junior midshipman. The senior snotties who had only come to sea a few months before us were all public-school entry and some years older. We considered, however, that the much longer training which we had done more than made up for the gap in our ages and we always looked upon ourselves as their equals.

We took it in turns to be duty wonk (junior midshipmen were known as wonks) and this was a day when you had to be particularly alert to avoid trouble. The duties included calling the sub, running his bath and seeing that he got up, being available at all times in the mess to run messages; dashing up on deck if the stove smoked to 'trim the Charley Noble', or in other words to turn the cowl on the stove pipe into the wind to prevent a down draught; being ready to jump up and light the sub's cigarette and in fact to act as general dog's body. You might be sitting on the settee in the dog watches reading or writing up some lecture notes (the junior midshipmen were never allowed to sit in the armchairs) when someone would shout 'Duty Wonk, t on the p.' (meaning Tune on the Phone).

Up you would jump, wind up the gramophone, put in a new needle – choose a record you liked and start up. Before you could sit down again there would be a roar, 'Not that damned tune you bloody wonk, put on…so and so." The seniors all had their particular musical likes and you were well advised to learn what they were. Once started you might be playing the p for half an hour trying your best to please the majority.

When asked a question you were never allowed to say, 'I don't know' unless you quickly added, 'but I will find out.' Then off you would dash to find the answer or hope that if you stayed away long enough the matter would be forgotten. If asked, 'Why did you do this?' or 'Why didn't you do that?' never start your explanation with 'I thought' because you would then immediately be asked 'What happened to the man who thought?' Whereupon you had to go down on your knees and recite the sad story of the man who thought and the three misfortunes which befell him in consequence, all of which are quite unprintable.

While still very new, a junior midshipman might be told to go and get the key of the starboard watch from the Quartermaster. Up he would go on deck and the Quartermaster, knowing the joke, would refer him perhaps to the Bosun who in turn would send him to the Captain of the Forecastle, or the Chief Stoker, or the Bandmaster, or the Captain of the Heads and so on endlessly until at last the unfortunate lad realised that the whole thing was a leg pull.

Certain silly bits of backchat were invented by our seniors for their amusement and we had always to be ready with the appropriate response. One which sticks in my memory is this:

'Utting,' someone would shout, Why Utting and not Hutton I do not remember.
  'Sir, would answer Hutton, springing to his feet.
  'What's the use of you?'
  'None bugger all FA Sir,' he would reply.

He would then resume his seat amid shouts of laughter. This little pantomime might be repeated almost daily and never failed to raise peals of hearty laughter, which suggests that we were very easily amused in those days. Incidentally, this same young officer had a very distinguished record as a Captain in the Second War and eventually rose to flag rank.

On guest nights we were sometimes expected to amuse our seniors and their guests by carrying out evolutions. Without saying a word the sub would raise his fork and push it into the bell cord overhead. This was 'Fork in the beam' and meant that all the wonks must make a dash for the door and get out of the mess. 'Bumph' meant a mad rush to the officer heads to return with one piece of lavatory paper untorn and uncreased. 'Dogs of war out… so and so' and out he had to be thrown, kicking and struggling, by our combined efforts. There were others such as 'Creep for Jesus' and 'Bitters crawl', but it would take too long to describe them all. The last to complete an evolution would get one or more cracks over the backside, but on the other hand the first home was often rewarded with a glass of port. If at any time the Sub said 'Breadcrumbs' the junior midshipman had to stuff their fingers in their ears and shut their eyes. Something was going to be said that was not considered fit for the ears of the young gentlemen. Woe betide you if on hearing the shout 'Negative Breadcrumbs', you looked up, as this revealed that you had not stopped your ears properly. You had to wait until you were banged on the head.

Shortly after our arrival we were 'Christened'. This ceremony took place after dinner on a guest night. One by one we had to kneel in front of the sub with a ship's biscuit balanced on our head and sing the christening hymn, 'Lord of Power and Lord of Night at this festival tonight'… to a well-known tune from *Ancient and Modern*. When we reached the line, 'Till the hand of grace comes down' the sub brought his fist down with a tremendous bang, breaking the biscuit and nearly knocking us out in the process. The last lines then had to be sung fortissimo, 'Alleluia let us sing, hail to this our Christening'.

It was not always hard work and hard knocks on guest nights, however. Often they were good fun with the band playing in the Flat outside, a glass or two of sherry beforehand, wine bill permitting, a glass of port with 'The King' and permission to smoke afterwards. The evening generally ended up with a sing-song round the piano or races over, through and round the chairs or competitive games like pushing a penny as far as possible with both feet behind a line and only one hand on the deck. We were soon taught all the bawdy gun room songs and jokes and we learned to drink, sometimes I regret to

Three Battleships: HMS Indomitable, HMS Inflexible, HMS Invincible

Fifteen Midshipman

say, to excess, and to smoke. And all this before we were quite sixteen. Regrettable as this may seem, I do not think it did any of us very much harm, and we kept ourselves reasonably fit with occasional games of rugger and hockey and plenty of golf and deck hockey, not to mention that daily dozen at early morning PT on the forecastle.

Apart from these activities our everyday life on board gave us plenty of exercise. If sent on a message you could stand still just long enough to say, 'Ay, Ay, Sir,' and then you had to FLY, and never must you be seen walking up or down a ladder; it must always be taken at the run. This insistence on everything being done at top speed or faster nearly resulted in a nasty accident. At general quarters one day the midshipman of P turret was sent to get something from the gun room. Dropping out of the rear door of the turret he dashed across the quarter deck and jumped down the main hatch meaning to negotiate the ladder to the deck below in the usual two strides. Only as he jumped did he see that the ladders had been removed at the main deck coaming which broke his fall slightly and he landed on the armoured hatch below, which luckily was closed. Very shaken, he picked himself up, completed his mission and returned to the turret. He was lucky to suffer nothing more serious than severe water on the knee. It is worth mentioning, perhaps, particularly in view of my later remarks about our captains, that when this accident occurred Captain Kennedy showed great kindness and consideration. He insisted that the midshipman in question should be put to bed in his starboard sleeping cabin instead of being sent ashore to hospital as at first proposed by the PMO.

Every Sunday morning before breakfast the junior midshipmen had to clean the bright work in the gun room. This was a chore we really detested because having to put on our best suit and clean shirt and collar ready for Sunday divisions we then had to get ourselves thoroughly dirty and untidy with our hands black from the Bluebell polish and our clothes covered in bits of cotton waste. Avoidance of this duty, however, could only be carried out at considerable risk because if bowled out, unless a very good excuse was forthcoming, the penalty would be severe. There was quite a lot of brasswork in the mess and if it was not all shining brightly when the sub made his inspection there was sure to be trouble and we would expect to hear the ominous words, 'All the young gentlemen will report to me in the gun room after divisions.'

We were lucky in having an exceptionally nice lot of ward room officers who took a great interest in us and who were most kind and helpful. They frequently asked us in for a drink or a meal. How we used to enjoy Sunday supper in the ward room with a cinema show or a game of bridge to follow. A guest-night dinner was even better. It would always develop into a most hilarious affair. There might be dancing in the ward room flat, or our Snotties' nurse, who was a great comedian, would amuse everyone by conducting the band or giving us one of his brilliant imitations of Harry Tate.

In marked contrast was the seeming indifference shown by our captains. (There were three during my time in the ship.) Here perhaps my memory is at fault, but I do not think there was any contact between the captain and the midshipman. We were never asked into the cuddy for a meal and in fact he seldom spoke to us except to give us an order or send us on a message. Captains and admirals in those days were remote and mysterious people, who did not consider it necessary to establish a personal contact with those under their command and who, in consequence, were seldom seen. There was no attempt to keep ship's companies informed of what was going on and there was never an occasion, that I can recall, that the captain fell the men in to give them a pep talk. During my two years only once did we see Admiral Beatty; not even after Jutland, when it might have been expected that he would visit all his ships. At the time this caused no surprise and I can only suppose that admirals were not expected to do that sort of thing. How different it is today.

Because, as midshipmen, we were still under training, our parents, even in wartime, had to pay the Admiralty £50 a year to supplement our meagre 1/9d. a day pay. This extraordinary arrangement was brought to an end through a question in Parliament arising from a parent, whose young son had been killed at Jutland, receiving afterwards a reminder from the Admiralty that the £50 payment was overdue. I think we used to draw about £6 a month. Nevertheless, after paying our mess bill, we were able to afford quite frequent trips to Edinburgh and the local golf course with occasional visits to cinemas and theatres, which shows how far a few pounds went in those days.

Being under eighteen we were not allowed to smoke or drink spirits, but we were allowed a 10/- wine bill, which went quite a long way with port and sherry at 2d. a glass, Marsala at 1 and a half pennies, Gin, which of course we were forbidden, was only a penny. a tot, and it was always full tots in those days no halves or thirds as became customary later on. When on occasions I was asked if I would like a gin, I always accepted fearing ridicule if I refused, and I would drink it down as if to the manner born, trying to disguise the fact that I found the taste quite disgusting. Gin was always Plymouth Gin. I do not remember how long it took to acquire the taste. A tin of fifty Gold Flake cigarettes cost only 1/3d. and on guest nights the junior midshipmen were allowed to smoke after 'The King'. I well remember buying my first pipe in Edinburgh, filling it up with strong ship's tobacco and lighting it up at the next guest night. Long before it was finnished I had to retire to the heads to be very sick.

The midshipmen's flat or staff flat as it was called, was forward, extending right across the ship with a square port each side, a skylight overhead and a ladder on to the upper deck. Another ladder led down to the cabin flat and deck below. Like all midshipmen's flats conditions were pretty crowded, with fifteen or more chests jammed one against the other and with little or no space between our hammocks, which were slung overhead at night.

I have vivid memories of that flat at sea in rough weather. The horrible fuggy smell which soon permeated the whole ship when battened down; the sound of water slopping from side to side as the ship pitched and rolled (the hatch and skylight were never quite watertight in heavy weather); the crash overhead as a green sea broke on the forecastle and the lurch as the bows were thrown up, up, up and then fell back with a sickening plunge, which made your stomach fall as if it had been left behind, bringing up with an almighty bump on the next oncoming wave. Amid all this heaving and tossing, being called to go on to watch at night and struggling out of your hammock followed by oaths and abuse from your neighbour whose hammock you had inadvertently clutched in an effort to retain some sort of balance. A frantic search for oilskin, sweater, scarf, gloves and sea boots, with feet getting wetter and colder all the time and a stomach beginning to turn over, hoping you could get up into the fresh air before being sick.

In harbour it was a very different scene. With hatch, skylight, and ports open the flat was light and airy. The noise, however, was scarcely less, the only difference being that instead of coming from the elements outside it came from the throats of the young gentlemen inside. There were those of us who were reasonably careful of our clothes and possessions and there were others who seemed to lose and mislay everything. The result was that the latter were always borrowing and the former, somewhat reluctantly, lending. At the times when the flat was full, for instance when we were getting ready to go ashore, there was much shouting, laughing and joking. Arguments generally ending in personal abuse and sometimes in a full-blooded scrap which might be finally settled by some hard bargaining over the fair price for some borrowed article of clothing. A watch kept, the price of a tea in Edinburgh, a glass, perhaps two glasses of sherry? In the middle of this pandemonium two blasts on the fog horn would be heard and with shouts of 'My God, two Gs, we are going to miss the boat' there would be a slamming of chests and a mad rush for the hatch and the flat would suddenly become empty and silent.

When in harbour we had instruction in seamanship, navigation, signals, torpedo, gunnery and engineering. Our Snotties' nurse as I have said was an amazing character and was full of little sayings which he would bring out during his seamanship lectures. 'Seamanship,' he would say to us, 'is the application of common sense to the everyday happenings of maritime existence.' When one of us sat silent trying to think of the answer to some question, he would remark, 'Silence is golden, but it cuts no ice.' When not under instruction we carried out the usual midshipman duties such as watchkeeping, running boats and divisional work.

On our first arrival in the *Indomitable* there was no Naval Instructor in the ship and so from time to time we were sent over to the *Indefatigable* for instruction in navigation and mathematics by the chaplain who was also a qualified NI. In those days it was quite usual for the Padre to combine both duties. Early in 1916 a young newly enrolled NI joined us. He was a shy studious type who had probably led a very sheltered existence and his introduction to life at sea must have been a real shock to his system. He used to be unmercifully ragged by his messmates in the ward room and I am afraid he was teased with little respect by the midshipmen who use to pull his leg most cruelly. He took all this with extreme good humour, however, and soon became very well liked though still remaining rather a figure of fun. He subsequently rose to the top of his branch and on retirement took holy orders.

At sea we were in three watches, acting as look-outs in the fore top by day and as assistant 4-inch gun and searchlight control officers by night. We were also available for bridge duties and at least twice a night we had to get cocoa for the officers on watch and at the end of the watch it was our job to go below and call the reliefs. How well I remember climbing up the outside ladder to the fore top in bad weather, clinging on for dear life as the ship rolled about and the full force of the wind caught you. With a stern wind the climb was sheer agony. You tried to hold your breath as clouds of hot funnel smoke swirled round you. At some point you probably had to open your mouth and take a breath and in with it came, in a great choking gulp, a lung full of the filthy stuff that left you coughing and gasping. On finally reaching the top you pushed open the small trap hatch and struggled through; no easy task when wearing an oilskin over an overcoat over countless sweaters. I wonder how many caps I lost overboard in my many journeys up and down that mast.

I remember too the trips to the galley at night for cocoa. Dodging under the swaying hammocks, trying to keep your feet and balance the jug of cocoa as the ship rolled, and the smell and the heat and the steam in the galley which was enough to turn the strongest stomach. Calling reliefs required much perseverance and a special technique. Woe betide you if a relief was late but also God help you if you broke the calling rules. Never, never must you shake or even touch an officer or shout at him. Switch on the light, call him by name, and tell him the time and report the weather, and repeat this until he is awake, then return over and over again until you see him out of his bunk.

When at four hours notice for steam, afternoon leave was granted to officers from 1 to 6.30 p.m. On Sundays and on make-and-mend afternoons those midshipmen not required for duty on board could go ashore in the one o'clock boat to spend the afternoon in Edinburgh or to play golf at one of the many nearby courses or for a game of hockey or rugger on the South Queensferry grounds. Buses ran from Hawes Pier to Edinburgh and returned in time to catch the 6.30 boat and trains ran from Dalmeny Station. Owing to the petrol shortage the buses ran on gas which was contained in a great bag attached to the roof which billowed and flapped about in a most alarming way when the gas was nearly expended.

An afternoon in Edinburgh might start with a visit to Gieves for a haircut or some other shopping, and then along to the King's Theatre for a matinée or the New Cinema in Princes Street where a continuous programme would be in progress, and then tea. There was a popular tea room at the cinema where for 1/6d. you could eat as many cakes and sandwiches as you liked. A really good money's worth. Finally into the bus at the Mound at 6 o'clock for the return to Queensferry. Midshipmen generally did this trip standing up as heaven help them if they did not jump up and offer their seat to their seniors.

There would be the occasional afternoon dance for junior officers at the Kintore Rooms arranged by the Edinburgh ladies. If there were not enough volunteers for these events some of us were detailed off to attend and did so very reluctantly, at least I know I did, because at that age I was shy, I was very uncertain of my dancing, and I was terrified of strange girls. I once appeared on the stage of the King's Theatre. Lady Beatty had arranged a charity matinée and the *Indomitable* was asked to provide a turn. Four of the smallest of us midshipman and two of the watchkeepers of much the same height, dressed ourselves in sailors No.6 uniforms and danced the hornpipe which we had rehearsed most diligently on board beforehand. I do not remember who our teacher was but the dance was a great success on the day.

We were all keen golfers and spent many enjoyable afternoons on Barnton or Bruntsfield links. A round which, thanks to the kindness of the members, was free, was followed by a slap-up tea in the clubhouse and then perhaps a game of billiards while putting off time before the arrival of the bus.

A well-known and very senior officer was often to be seen on the links always followed by his coxswain carrying just two clubs which he referred to as the pusher and the puncher. His voice could be heard booming across the fairway telling his coxswain to hand him the pusher or the puncher as the case might be. The pusher was a mashie which he used through the green and the puncher was a cleek with which he drove and putted. In spite of carrying such a limited armament he was a very difficult man to beat. I wonder what he would have thought of the modern golfer with his trolley and his matched irons and his bag with anything up to fourteen clubs in all.

Married officers in the Battle Cruiser Forces were fortunate in being able to see something of their wives, many of whom lived in houses or rooms in and around Edinburgh and South Queensferry. We midshipmen received many kindnesses and many good teas from the *Indomitable* wives. How much better off we were than our comrades in the ships of the Grand Fleet swinging round their anchors in Scapa Flow.

As far as I can remember there was occasional shore leave for chief and petty officers, but the sailors were only allowed ashore to the dockyard canteen on Saturday afternoons. Beer tickets were sold on board and were strictly rationed, but even so the men always seemed to get very drunk and the midshipman in charge of the motor launch bringing on these canteen parties had his work cut out to maintain order and discipline.

Running a picket boat was a wonderful experience, and a duty which every midshipman enjoyed. No modern motor boat will ever match the beauty, elegance and dignity of the old steam picket boat with its sparkling bright work, scrubbed wooden decks and spotless paintwork. Every midshipman took a proper pride in his boat's appearance and each week he would be expected to give the coxswain an extra tin or two of Bluebell polish. The crew consisted of a petty officer coxswain, two bowmen, a stern sheetman, a fender man, a stoker in the boiler room and a stoker petty officer in the engine room. When a midshipman was in the boat he always took the wheel himself and worked the engine-room gong while the coxswain stood alongside keeping a watchful eye open. There was an excellent understanding between midshipman and coxswain. The young inexperienced officer was in charge but the older and greatly experienced petty officer was there at his side to help and give advice if required, and this relationship was accepted gratefully on the one side and without any resentment on the other.

The boats were capable of nearly fifteen knots and it was a great thrill to handle them. Beware, however, of becoming careless or negligent. Inadvertently cross a senior officer's bows; pass too close to another ship without easing down so causing damage to a boat lying at boom or gangway with your wash; misjudge your alongside and crash the boat and ladder, and on return you would receive a blast from the OOW or the Commander which in all probability would be followed by a painful interview with the sub in the gun room.

I remember very vividly the 6.30 officers, trip from Hawes Pier on days when leave had been granted, particularly in the winter when it was dark. All the picket boats of the Fleet would be waiting at the pier, one alongside the other, having come in stern first in order to make a quick getaway, and each with its illuminated sign displayed on the top of the cabin. As the buses arrived down from Edinburgh the officers would stream on board their boats, one by one, and starting with the outside boat would then be off and away. With the engine opened right out, the whole boat throbbing and vibrating, the boiler-room fan roaring and sparks flying out of the funnels, a dozen or more boats would go dashing away towards the ships lying a mile or two distant. The midshipmen and boat's crew always looked on this return trip as a race and tried desperately to catch or out-distance the rest. The 56-foot boats belonging to the 3 Battle Squadron (the K.E.VII class) lying farther up the river were faster than the newer, but rather shorter, boats of the Battle Cruisers and always managed to draw away ahead, but there was never much to choose between the rest. In the excitement of the race, the midshipman could become very unpopular with his messmates sitting huddled up on the top of the cabin if he failed to ease down when the spray started to come over or if a sudden alteration of course brought water slopping in over the officers in the stern sheets.

In addition to the two picket boats the *Indomitable* carried a steam pinnace, generally known as the steam bus. She was an ugly stocky little boat with a small cabin aft and the wheel up for'ard before the funnel. She was not very fast and was therefore generally used for all the dirty work such as landing working parties, bringing off stores with the pinnace or cutter in tow or towing the motor

Silver Boxing Cups competed for by the crew of HMS Indomitable

HMS Indomitable

launch when, as often as not, its engine had broken down; and particular duty which always came her way was that of DSB (Duty Steam Boat). A turn of duty in the steam pinnace was not as popular with us midshipmen as running a picket boat but it gave us plenty of work and experience. A DSB trip, for instance, started at 8 o'clock; a call had to be made alongside each of the Battle Cruisers for their correspondence, then to the *Columbine* for letters from the destroyers, then up stream to the light cruisers and the 3 Battle Squadron lying off Charlestown and finally down again to the *Lion* to deliver all the correspondence so collected. Back to the ship for a short dinner hour and then off again to be alongside the *Lion* by 1 o'clock to embark a marine orderly with all the flagship's outgoing correspondence for distribution. The forenoon trip would then be repeated again. Battle Cruisers, *Columbine*, Light Cruisers and 3 Battle Squadron., eventually returning to the *Lion* to drop the orderly and so back to the ship for tea. As likely as not in the dog watches a signal would "Send DSB to flagship" and off you would go to the *Lion* again wondering what was required this time.

The weather made all the difference on these long DSB trips. If it was fine and calm all was plain sailing. If there was a fog (and there was plenty of it in the Forth) you had an anxious time groping your way from ship to ship in a strong tide with little to guide you but the sound of their bells and a somewhat unreliable compass. When it blew hard and when the tide turned against the wind the result was a very nasty choppy sea into which the little steam pinnace would drive, burying her nose in the oncoming waves up for'ard with only a small weather shield for protection.

Coming back from one such trip late in the evening, very wet and thoroughly chilled, I turned in but woke up next morning feeling very ill indeed. I was pushed off hurriedly ashore to hospital where it was found that I was suffering from pleurisy and double pneumonia. This was pretty serious because in those days there were no modern antibiotics and drugs, and for some time I was very dangerously ill. Being young and strong, however, I soon pulled through and when on recovery I was sent on ten days' sick leave it all seemed almost worthwhile. It was worthwhile. It was decided on board that this had happened because I had gone away in the boat

at night without enough warm clothes on and strict orders were issued to the OOW's to see that in future midshipmen going away in boats were suitably and adequately clad.

There was a great temptation to try and show what a brilliant and dashing boat handler you were. To make a good alongside at high speed, judging the tide to a nicety and pulling up with a smother of foam under your counter as you rang down full astern was a way of demonstrating your skill, but it did not always come off. A small error of judgement could result in a crash which could easily damage your boat, or if a strong tide was running, getting your bows either swept in and firmly wedged under the ladder or carried out while the bowmen desperately struggled to hold on to the boat rope. In any case a very undignified and un-seamanlike situation, which could have been avoided with a little more care and attention and if you had not been so anxious to show off.

Several incidents come vividly to mind when recalling my gun room days. The most memorable of all was the Battle of Jutland, but there is no room here to describe that in detail. I might mention, however, the unforgettable sight of the Grand Fleet at sea, as seen from the Battle Cruisers on any of the exercises we used to carry out. At first just columns of smoke on the horizon. Then the cruisers spread ahead on the AK line would come into sight and then, at last, this huge armada of anything up to thirty battleships advancing in five or more columns surrounded by a close screen of destroyers. This was a spectacle the like of which will never be seen again.

I well remember the day that our No. 2 sub lieutenant was killed in a turret. The turret's crew were at drill and they were exercising loading by hand. At 850 lb practice projectile had been lifted out of the use bin in the gun house and was being swung towards the loading tray when it slipped out of the grab and fell down the gun-loading hoist into the working chamber below, a drop out of about ten feet. Sub-Lieutenant Thompson, who was standing at the bottom of the hoist, had no time to jump clear and was hit by falling shell and killed instantly. Much as we junior midshipmen disliked the chap we were shocked and appalled when we heard of this accident and his death cast a gloom over the gunroom for many days.

Then there was the occasion when, while undergoing engineering instruction, another midshipman and I, who should have been tracing steam pipes in the engine room, decided to climb up inside to the top of the foremost funnel, thinking that from this vantage point we would have an excellent view of the sailors getting out the torpedo net defence; an exercise which we hoped would provide us with some amusement. Needless to say the boilers below were out and the funnel was cold and clear of smoke. As we were climbing to the top, dense smoke suddenly started to come up from below. Unknown to us the diesel dynamo had been started up. Down we scrambled as fast as we could go but in the darkness and smoke we could not find the door through which we had entered the funnel casing. Now thoroughly alarmed, we started to shout and bang on the side of the funnel and eventually we were heard, the diesel was stopped, and we were able to find our way out. Why we were not punished for this foolish escapade I cannot imagine. Perhaps in the general confusion we managed to slip out unseen and return to the engine room undetected. Perhaps our Engineer Instructor was a kind-hearted man who decided to overlook the matter. In any case, we were both very lucky for had it come to the ears of the Commander I am sure we both would have received a good thrashing.

Another memory is of a gun room picnic party away under sail in the captain's galley. When trying to land at Bo'ness pier the helmsman completely misjudged his alongside and the boat was swept by the strong tide right under the pier. Before we could unship and lower the masts both were caught and snapped off short at the thwarts. This disaster completely spoiled our picnic and we had plenty of time to try and think up some excuses and wonder what sort of punishment awaited us during a long and exhausting pull back to the ship. To our intense relief and surprise, the captain treated the whole matter as a great joke and we got off scot-free.

Again, I well remember a combined ward room and gun room picnic at Scapa Flow with a tremendous meal of bangers and bacon fried up on a large fire and much singing and a vast consumption of sloe gin in the launch on the return journey. Little did we think at the time that within forty eight hours we would be in the thick of the Battle of Jutland.

Looking back it would seem that for the Battle Cruisers Force, at any rate, the war at sea over 1915-16 was fought at a very leisurely tempo. During the eight months from the time I joined the *Indomitable* to the Battle of Jutland, we only did thirty-three days at sea, and, moreover, because at the time the submarine threat in the North Sea was slight and the air threat non-existent, it was possible, when at sea, to maintain a very easy three-watch defence organisation. It was only necessary to assume a higher state of readiness on the rare occasions that contact with enemy surface ships was expected. Since no practice facilities were available in the Firth of Forth, firings had to be carried out either from Invergordon or Scapa. The result was that in the same eight months we only fired our main armament four times and our secondary armament once. In the circumstances it is hardly surprising that the gunnery of the Battle Cruisers at Jutland was poor. Our anchorage above the Forth Bridge provided ships with complete protection, and consequently when in harbour ship's companies had absolute relaxation, and as far as the officers were concerned, plenty of leave in very civilised surroundings. How different from the 1939/45 war when ships spent long periods at sea with only short rests in harbour and when, owing to the constant submarine and air threat, a very high degree of readiness had to be maintained at all times in harbour as well as at sea.

I think that the lot of the junior midshipmen was probably harder in the war because, owing to restricted levels and general boredom when in harbour, the senior gunroom officers found their amusement in bullyragging the young gentlemen. The sub of the mess had great power which he could easily abuse and I do not think that many captains, commanders or senior wardroom officers worried much about what methods were used so long as the behaviour and general discipline of the gunroom was good. One or two extreme cases of bullying came to light leading to official enquiries and disciplinary action, and as a result the harshness of gunroom life was gradually eased. It must be remembered, however, that it was traditional that continual chasing and much chastisement was an essential part of a young officer's upbringing. It never did anyone much harm unless carried to extremes and it certainly kept us young chaps up

Postcard of HMS Indomitable

Officers and Midshipmen of HMS Indomitable

Appendix Four: Midshipman Rogerson

to the mark. There was here a danger, however, that these methods instilled into officers at a very early age too high a regard for, and obedience to, authority, a too strongly developed sense of the importance of rank and seniority resulting in the reluctance of junior officers to express their own opinions and a too ready unquestioning acceptance of those of their seniors. Perhaps it tended to stifle initiative and fresh ideas and produce a tradition of rigid conformity.

Great social changes have taken place in the country as a result of two world wars and these changes are reflected in the modern navy, where conditions and attitudes today are very different from those that I have described. It should be remembered, however, that the old system, with all its faults, produced the admirals and senior officers of the Second World War, many of whom proved themselves to be brilliant and inspiring leaders.

Jutland

I was a midshipman aged sixteen in HMS *Indomitable* at the Battle of Jutland and these are some personal memories of the battle. The 3 Battle Cruiser Squadron consisting of the *Invincible*, flagship of Rear Admiral the Hon. Horace Hood, the *Indomitable* and the *Inflexible*, had arrived at the Scapa from Rosyth on May 23 1916 to carry out gunnery and torpedo exercises. The gunnery exercises were of particular importance for us as it was the first opportunity we had had to test out, and get acquainted with, the new director system which had just been installed at Rosyth.

At about 6.30 p.m. on the evening of Tuesday, 30 May, the signal was received to raise steam for 22 knots and at 9.30 the squadron sailed, followed by the whole of the Grand Fleet. We had no idea why we had been ordered out but undoubtedly there was a feeling of suppressed excitement on board as we passed through the Hoxa Gate in the fading light. On more than one occasion lately we had set out at high speed to intercept enemy ships which had been reported at sea but each time we had returned without making contact. What were the Germans up to? Were they indeed at last venturing out into the North Sea? Why had we put to sea so suddenly? Yes, I am sure there was a strong feeling that something was really afoot this time. I remember some of us junior midshipmen racing

up and down the quarter deck discussing among ourselves whether a midshipman had any chance of distinguishing himself in a modern fleet action and deciding probably not.

At 5 o'clock next morning, I went up to the foretop to keep the forenoon watch as submarine lookout, our squadron with two light cruisers and four screening destroyers, was steaming at a leisurely 14 knots and carrying out a normal zig-zag. We were ahead and out of sight of the Grand Fleet but from time to time we turned round to keep in touch. There seemed to be no sign of any urgency and last night's feeling of excitement ebbed away and I decided that this must be just another routine sweep into the North Sea.

This atmosphere of calm was suddenly shattered when at about 2.50 p.m. we intercepted *Galatea*'s first sighting report. From then on excitement steadily mounted as further signals came in with the news that the 1 and 2 BCS. were engaging the enemy battle cruisers and then that the 5 th battleship had joined in. The *Invincible* hoisted B J 1 – G 2 5, assume first degree readiness - speed 25 knots, shortly to be followed by B J – Action Stations. As we pushed on southwards, working up to our maximum speed, the thought uppermost in everyone's mind was 'Are we going to get there in time?' I may have felt some slight apprehension at the thought of going into action but the prevailing sensation was one of intense excitement. My action station was in the foretop as Dumaresq worker so that whatever was going to happen, I was going to have a grandstand view. I do not remember whether at our action stations we were given any information about how the battle was going or were even told that the High Seas Fleet had been sighted. We only know that we were doing our utmost to join Sir David Beatty and take up our proper place with him in the Battle Cruiser line. The engine room and boiler rooms threw in every ounce of steam and drove forward every revolution they could get. They did wonders and I believe the squadron worked up to 26 knots.

Even after this lapse of time certain incidents stand out in my memory but for details of times, courses and speeds I have had to refer to some brief notes which I made after the action. I should perhaps say something about the weather conditions which played such an important part in the battle. It was a calm but hazy day. Maximum visibility could not have been more than 12,000 yards while at times and in certain directions it was suddenly less than this. During the action visibility was still further reduced by the smoke from so many coal-burning ships steaming at high speed and I believe that at one time during the action we were firing with only 8,000 yards on the sights. These hazy conditions made ship identification, range-taking and spotting very difficult and it afforded the German Fleet protection since by turning away when the British fire became too hot they could quickly disappear from sight altogether. It must be said, however, that being to the eastward the British Fleet had the best of the poor light conditions during the last hours of daylight.

Soon after 5 o'clock the sound of distant gunfire was heard and at about 5.30 the *Chester* on our starboard beam was seen to open fire. Immediately the *Invincible* swung round to starboard and led the squadron towards her. Three German cruisers then came into sight broad on the port bow and we opened up on them with our main armament and they quickly turned away and vanished from sight. In turning they must have fired torpedoes at us for a few minutes later we sighted them approaching and all three ships took separate avoiding action. I clearly remember looking over the side of the foretop and seeing a torpedo passing slowly down our portside on the surface not more than ten yards away with its red war head and its propellers slowly revolving. It was obviously at the end of its run but a very near miss for all that. At the same time I saw the *Invincible* haul out to Starboard, and stop with all her safety valves lifting and a tremendous roar of steam and with the 'Disregard' flag flying. I thought, 'Oh God, she has been torpedoed.' But the next minute she hoisted Flag One (Line ahead) and hauling down 'Disregard' she led off to the westward again in the direction of heavy gun fire and we followed falling in behind the *Inflexible*.

It was now just after 6 o'clock and soon flashes of gunfire were visible ahead, and then the *Lion* appeared almost right ahead and steering towards us, with her guns firing to starboard, but still the enemy was hidden from sight in the haze. Then as the *Invincible* led round to port to bring the squadron into station ahead of the *Lion* suddenly the dim outline of four enemy ships loomed up

out of the haze. They were difficult to identify but we took them to be Battle Cruisers which in fact they were. As we turned to bring the enemy ships on our starboard beam, at about 10,000 yards, the squadron opened up with all its main armament guns. Our fire was quickly returned and soon shots were falling all round us.

As I have said our director firing system had just been installed and we had done only one test firing with it at Scapa a day or two before leaving. The gunnery officer therefore had a difficult decision to make. Should he use the new system which though more efficient was virtually untried, or should he revert to the old less accurate but well tested system of gunlayers firing? I remember he decided not to risk using the new director system and so throughout the action guns and turrets were individually laid and trained.

For about twenty minutes we were hotly engaged but I think I was too busy with my Dumaresq to feel frightened. I can remember the continuous ripple of flashes all along the enemy line but in the poor visibility the ships could never be seen clearly. I cannot say that I remember where our shots were falling although it is now known that the squadron firing was very good and that we were hitting the enemy hard. The noise of our guns I found very heartening and welcome as it helped to drown the rumbling noise made by the shells passing over us and the crack of those falling short, although the enormous columns of water thrown up were only too visible and sometimes uncomfortably close. We must have been constantly straddled at this time but not once were we or the *Inflexible* hit. Our only battle scar was a small hole in our foremost funnel, but a number of shell splinters came inboard indicating that some of the enemy's shells which fell short had burst on impact with the sea.

It was during this phase of the action and about 6.35 that the *Invincible* was hit by two shells in quick succession and blew up. Although only separated from her by the *Inflexible* nobody in the foretop saw the explosion or realised what had happened as we were all fully occupied with our fire-control duties. The first we knew of it was when close to starboard we passed the bows and stern of a ship sticking up out of the water about thirty feet and some half a dozen figures clinging to some wreckage. It was a grim and sad moment when seeing the name

Invincible on the stern portion we realised that we were passing all that remained of our flagship.

Shortly after this the enemy ships turned away and were lost to sight and although we altered course we could not regain contact. Then on orders from the *Lion* we turned round and took station astern of the other Battle Cruisers. It was only now that we realised that alas the *Queen Mary* and the *Indefatigable* were missing. At this point a disabled and motionless German cruiser appeared and received a broadside from each Battle Cruiser as it passed down the line and then faded from sight astern.

Some minutes later we saw the Grand Fleet coming into action astern. The ships could not be distinguished but through the haze and smoke could be seen what appeared to be one continuous line of flame from the flashes of their guns extending over an arc of about 60°, a truly tremendous sight. However, we hadn't much time to admire this display for enemy ships appeared again briefly and we became engaged once more. Simultaneously we saw a flotilla of German destroyers approaching on the starboard bow and as the big ships disappeared from sight again we shifted our fire to the destroyers and forced them to turn away under the cover of smoke.

At about 8.15 as the light was failing we had our last brief sighting and short burst of fire but we lost touch again and that was the end of the battle for us. We steamed southward throughout the night in company with Admiral Beatty and the rest of the Battle Cruisers remaining at action stations all the time. I was able to nip down to the gunroom for a few minutes to get a little food but spent the rest of the night in the foretop feeling very cold but too excited and worked up to sleep.

Sometime during the middle watch the tension was somewhat relieved and the silence was broken by a volley of oaths from the other side of the foretop. The cause of the commotion was the other foretop midshipman, now a retired admiral, who having struggled up the mast carrying a large jug of cocoa which he had obtained from the galley, tripped as he pushed up through the manhole and deposited the entire jug of hot cocoa over the rate officer who was huddled up on the floor of the top trying to get some sleep.

At about 3.30 just after daylight we turned north to join up with the C-in-C and the Battle

Fleet and a Zeppelin was sighted a long way astern. We hopefully fired off two rounds of 122 armour piercing but I don't suppose they went within miles of it. However, when some cruisers also opened fire, it turned away and was soon lost to sight. Early in the morning Admiral Beatty signalled to the Battle Cruisers, 'The losses on both sides have been heavy but we hope to cut off and annihilate the whole German Fleet today. It is up to every man to do his utmost.; Unknown to us at the time the German Fleet had slipped through astern of the Grand Fleet in the night and had by now regained the safety of its own waters. When this became known later in the day we turned for home. I remember when on watch in the afternoon passing through a large patch of oil and wreckage in which were floating a lot of dead fish and a number of dead bodies. We could not identify the uniforms and we hoped we were passing over the graveyard of some German ship but in all probability it was the spot where one of our Battle Cruisers had blown up.

We reached harbour early on the morning of 2 June and immediately started to take in 1400 tons of coal. Shortly afterwards I went into Rosyth dockyard to have a look at some of the ships which had been taken in for repairs. The *Warspite*, which had been heavily hit, seemed to have suffered most damage in the six-inch gun battery and at the base of the funnels where the plating was torn and buckled and blackened. The *Tiger*, though hit by ten big shells, did not show much outward signs of damage except for a large hole right through her after funnel.

On board the *Lion* I was taken to see the midship (Q) turret which had received three hits. There was a great hole in the front of the turret between the guns and part of the armoured roof plating had been lifted and twisted back. Everything in the gun house and working chamber was scorched and blackened by the fire which had started after the shells burst. Throughout the turret the horrid acrid smell of burned cordite seemed to cling to everything.

It was a terrible scene of devastation where all but two of the entire turret's crew had died, including a midshipman of my term who was in charge of the working chamber. The ship had been saved from complete destruction by the quick thinking and prompt action of the turret officer Captain Harvey, RMA, who though mortally wounded, managed to pass the order to the handing room to close the magazine doors and flood. When a few minutes later the flash from the ignited cordite in the gun house and working chamber passed down the trunk, there had just been time to seal off and flood the magazine, and although every man of the shell room and handing room crews was killed, the ship was saved from a terrible internal explosion similar to that which had destroyed the *Queen Mary*, *Indefatigable* and *Invincible*.

After the battle there was much speculation about the German losses. From all reports it was generally believed that they must have been as heavy, if not heavier, than ours. This proved to be wishful thinking and so when some time later the true facts became known we felt bitterly disappointed. Somehow we had missed our opportunity. We had allowed the German Fleet to slip through our fingers and instead of winning an overwhelming victory we had only achieved a partial success and in all probability we would never be given another chance.

Coaling the Battleship *Indomitable*

All ships of the Navy (except for destroyers, a small number of light cruisers and one squadron of battleships) were coal burners. Coaling was necessarily a frequent operation. It was always carried out immediately on return to harbour when anything up to 1,500 tons might be taken in, and also at regular intervals while in harbour further amounts of about 300 tons to keep bunkers topped up. During the eight months preceding the Battle of Jutland we coaled no less than thirty times. There cannot be many officers serving in the Navy today who have ever had to coal a ship.

The *Indomitable* in which I served as a midshipman from 1915-17 was far and away the best coaling ship in the Fleet. Admittedly the long flush deck extending from the forecastle to the after super-structure was a great advantage as it enabled us to use the collier's derricks at all four holds, a much faster method than using their own ship's derricks and the slower electric bollards. However, even in competition with the other Battle Cruisers which enjoyed the same advantages, we were always the first ship to finish and often our collier was shoving off when other ships were only halfway through the job. We seldom averaged less than 400

tons an hour and on one occasion according to my diary we took in 500 tons in just over an hour at an average rate of 474 tons per hour.

When coaling at Rosyth we always had the same collier, the *Rotherhill*, and this resulted in a great saving of time as the master knew exactly where to place his ship alongside (always on our starboard side) and the ship's company were familiar with all the gear and could quickly get the derricks rigged and everything ready for a quick start.

Coal-ship mornings provided a strange variety of dress. We midshipmen wore an overall suit over an old pair of trousers or football shorts, a rugger vest and, in the winter, probably a seaman's jersey for extra warmth. A cap cover on our heads, a scarf round our necks and an old pair of shoes or gymshoes and leather engine-room gloves. Wardroom officers generally wore in addition a very old monkey jacket with possibly some tattered remnants of stripes still adhering to the sleeves and a very old cap. The sailors looked like a lot of pirates in all sorts of fancy rigs, some in coloured football jerseys and shorts, some in old serge trousers and flannels with silks or coloured handkerchiefs tied round their heads. The chief petty officers and petty officers were generally dressed in overall suits, old caps and coats. But ranks and ratings were not easily distinguishable and as the work proceeded even faces became unrecognisable.

Preparation for coaling was made while entering harbour. The deck plates covering the coal chutes were removed and canvas chutes were rigged between decks. Q turrets were trained across the deck with guns at maximum elevation and bags, barrows, strops and shovels were brought up on deck. Each part of the ship was assigned to one of the collier's four holds and was organised into 5 or 6 gangs about 10 strong spaced out round the hole for digging the coal and filling the bags. A PO or leading hand worked the hook, with a midshipman on each winch and other midshipmen and boys for throwing empty bags back into the hold. The officer of Division with one of his POs was in general charge of the hold, watching every operation and keeping an eye on the standing and running rigging. Inboard, at each dump, was a party of about 10, mostly daymen dealing with the hoists as they arrived, getting the full bags away quickly on the barrows, which were worked by marines, and

King George V being greeted by Admiral Beatty at a parade held after the Battle of Jutland

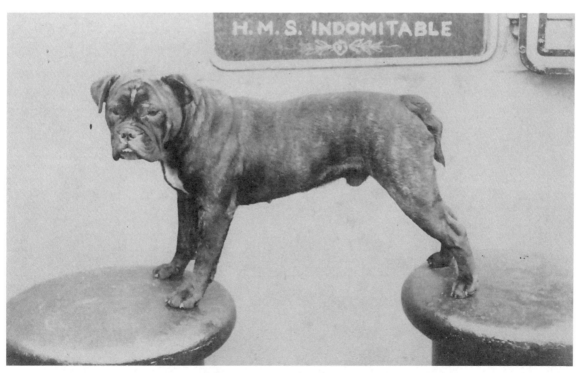

Buller, ships mascot, HMS Indomitable

Picnic on the shore, Scapa Flow

seeing that the deck was clear before the next hoist came swinging in. The full bags were rushed away to the top of the chutes by the barrowmen under the watchful eye of the captain of marines who was traffic controller and the empties brought back and returned to the hold. A selected number of bags had to be weighed so that an accurate estimate of the amount of coal coming in could be made. Stokers were stationed at the top of the chutes and below in the bunkers trimming the coal as it came down. Chutes could easily become jammed and it was very important to keep them clear and so ensure that coal did not pile up on the deck and cause blockages and delays. A careful count of the number of bags coming in was kept at each dump and it was the chaplain's coal-ship duty to act as one of these tallymen. Finally, there was the band. In the *Indomitable* at that time we had a Maltese band and I can see them now on a cold windy day huddled on top of the turret or in the superstructure, covered in coal dust, looking thoroughly miserable but blowing away manfully on their instruments and somehow managing to make themselves heard above the general noise and racket going on all around.

High-speed coaling needed great spirit and enthusiasm to sustain the prolonged and exhausting physical effort, particularly in the collier's holds. Good organisation and a high degree of training was also essential and this together with the determination to beat all the other ships was the key to our success in the *Indomitable*. As soon as the collier was secured alongside the hold, parties swarmed on board. Bags, shovels and strops were passed down and the gangs distributing themselves around the hold started at once to dig and fill up the bags. In the meantime, others were topping up and positioning the derricks with one plumbing the centre of the hold and one over the dump. Topping lifts were then belayed, all guys and preventer guys set up and the ends of the inhaul and whip were shackled to the big coaling hook. The midshipmen on the winches opened up the cylinder drain cocks and ran the engines in both directions with a great hissing of steam and clanking of pistons to clear the cylinders of water and then looked to see that the wire on the winch drums was clear of riding turns and free to run. As the first hoist swung inboard the 'Advance' was sounded by the bugler, the band struck up, the time was noted and coaling had started. With the

rattle and clank of six steam winches working flat out, the rumble of the barrows trundling the bags away on deck and the swish and bang as the hosts of 15 to 20 bags came slamming down on deck, the noise was terrific. Coal dust blew thicker and thicker over everything and everyone, getting into eyes and down throats. The smell of coal was everywhere, and the taste of coal in everyone's mouth.

There was an ordered sequence of events which was repeated over and over again in each hold and on deck. The hook man standing on a pinnacle of coal in the middle of the hold waited for the hook to be lowered and then seizing it he plunged down with it into the gloom of the hold towards the gang whose turn it was, and who had just stropped up a hoist of some fifteen two-hundred weight bags. The two ends of the strop were shackled over the hook and a blast on the whistle told the midshipman on the whip that all was ready below. With his lever to heave in he now cracks open the steam valve to tighten the whip and take the weight. 'Right away' comes the shout from below and giving the winch a bit more steam the hoist is slowly pulled from the side or corner of the hold up the slope of coal until it is directly under the derrick head. Now the steam valve is opened wide, the winch heaves in at full speed, and the hoist rises up out of the hold. Meanwhile, the inhaul winch is taking up the slack and as the hoist clears the hold the inhaul wire is taughtened. This is where the winch workers have to exercise some nice judgement. When high enough the whip winch is stopped and the inhaul winch heaves at full speed. The two wires tauten out quickly and the hoist is pulled out towards the ship. Now is the moment: the midshipman on the whip winch takes his foot off the brake, slams his lever off, opens up the throttle and walks back full speed. The hoist comes inboard with a tremendous swing and when over the dump the inhaul winch is 'let go' and the bags fall with a crash on deck.

The dump party quickly gets round the hoist and unhooks one end of the strop, the winches heave in again, the strop unreeves through the beckets and strop and hook come swinging back over the hold to be lowered again into the hook-worker's hand. By this time the next gang have their hoist stropped up and ready for lifting, and the whole process is repeated over again. The hook must never be kept waiting in the hold and as each hoist arrives the dump party must work like mad to get the bags barrowed away and the deck clear to receive the next hoist which must on no account be delayed.

The whole operation was carried out at top speed and everyone had to be alert and active if they were to avoid danger. An error on the part of the winchman and the hoist might swing wildly and dangerously across the hold or land too far inboard and if at the shout of 'stand clear' you didn't move quickly you were for it. An empty bag might have been carried up across one of the wires to be flung high in the air as the wire suddenly tautened and woe betide anyone who didn't jump clear. The iron beckets on the bag could easily cut a man's head open. A large knob of coal could suddenly be jerked from an overfull bag as the hoist is swung inboard. 'Stand from under' everyone shouted and those in danger dived for cover.

Like all evolutions at sea, it is practice and training which enable men to carry out difficult operations at high speed and at the same time with safety. Thanks to good drill, good judgement and quick reactions to danger it was seldom that any serious accident occurred during 'Coal Ship'.

The end of coaling was announced by the 'Cease Fire' on the bugle and this was always greeted by a tremendous cheer from the holds of the collier. The exhausted gangs would fling down their shovels and start to climb up out of the dust and dirt, emerging completely black from head to foot. All full bags were hoisted in and then shovels and empties were stropped up and this made up the last hoist. Derricks were then replaced, everybody came inboard and the collier shoved off.

There was keen rivalry between the parts of the ship with the main top division nearly always coming out on top. This was hardly surprising however as they had the widest part of the deck for their dump and could therefore swing the hoists in and get the bags cleared away more quickly.

As soon as the collier shoved off the cleaning up started and the sailors would be busy with hoses and brooms and paintwork clothes for another hour at least. The officers, however, all repaired to the ward room where the wine steward handed round trays of soda water cocktails. I can still remember the taste of those drinks which as a young midshipman I thought quite revolting but of course I swallowed them down pretending to enjoy them. After that off to the gun room bathroom where with soap and hot water in our little hip baths we eventually scrubbed ourselves clean except for a black rim of coal dust round our eyes. This had to be removed later on in the chest flat with a handkerchief and a good application of Vaseline. By dinner time the ship and everyone in it was clean, a make-and-mend was piped and another coal ship was over.

Scrapbook,
Fresh generation and Family groups

I don't believe in magic, the young boy said. The old man smiled, you will, when you see her.
Atticus

City Rogersons. From left: Andrea Rogerson, Carole Rogerson, Dinah Rogerson, Jeremy Rogerson, Tessa Rogerson, Nico Rogerson

Four Rogersons, from left Mark, Jeremy, Barnaby and David

Cousins in the Eland office attic: back row from left: Sam Rogerson, Mathew Rogerson, Barnaby Rogerson, David Rogerson and Patrick Wills: seated from left, Mary Lou Hussey, Lucy Knollys, Jennifer Wills

Jeremy Rogerson (left) with his sister Jane and brother Peter

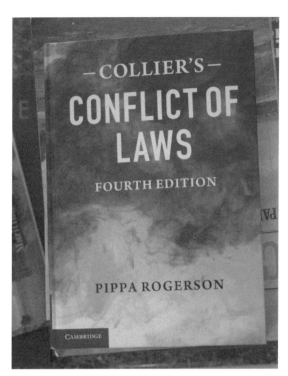

Book cover, Pippa Rogerson

Louis Stapleton, son of Diana Rogerson

"I want some cousins in top hats" James, Keith, Barnaby and Kathy obediently spruced up for Annabelle Rogersons wedding on 8 June

Lili taking a fence, Co Galway

Lucy Rogerson, Mrs Porter with some of her sons

Mathew Rogerson and daughter Lucy

Mary Lou Rogerson, Mrs Francis Hussey between her two daughters, Sophie and Sasha

Molly Rogerson on the morning of her graduation

Mr and Mrs John Rogerson

Mr and Mrs Sam Rogerson

Pippa Rogerson and her five Fitzsimon daughters; Olivia, Harriet, Beatrice, Izzy and Milly

Family of Kathy Rogerson gathered for her funeral, May 17, 2014. From left back row; Frank, Corinna, Molly, Carlotta, Hannah, Rose, Luke, Louis, Django and Nico. Front row, lurcher, Barnaby, Dido, David and Shamos.

Cheers from Sam Rogerson

Barnaby Hugh Rogerson (born 1960), son of Cdr Keith Rogerson

About the Author

Barnaby Rogerson was educated at Cottesmore (aged seven to thirteen) and was just beginning to enjoy his time at Charterhouse when he was expelled, so took his A levels at Peter Symonds College at Winchester. A degree in History from St Andrews University proved to be adequate preparation for work as a barman, tutor for a child star in a film made on a Greek island and a pony boy on a Highland estate. He also worked for two independent publishers in Chichester which led to a job in the press department of the Afghanistan Support Committee.

He then wrote a guidebook to Morocco, followed by one on Tunisia and then Istanbul (both co-written with Rose Baring) then one on Cyprus. His first proper history book was a *Travellers History of North Africa*, which was followed by *The Prophet Muhammad* (a biography), then an account of the early Caliphate, *The Heirs of the Prophet*. These early successes were followed by *The Last Crusaders*: an attempt to simultaneously tell the story of the 150 year-long war fought between Christian Portugal and Muslim Morocco, interwoven with the rise of Hapsburg Spain and the Ottoman Empire, whose resulting conflict spread across the globe. The fall of Granada and Constantinople being just the first notes that inexorably conclude with the titanic clashes at Lepanto, Famagusta and the Battle of the Three Kings. So that we see that the very last of the Crusades transforms itself into the first two colonial Empires, (1415–1580). It was an ambitious project.

In between these various books, Barnaby worked as a lecturer with tour groups, as a freelance journalist and started a small reprint business called Sickle Moon Books. This latter venture should have been doomed but instead led to an invitation to takeover Eland Publishing Ltd, with a well-established backlist of classic travel books. For the last twenty years, Barnaby has run Eland with his wife Rose Baring, whilst they also brought up two daughters in London. To add variety to all this shared job and childcare, Rose re-trained as a psychoanalytical psychotherapist.

Barnaby also continues to write. *Rogerson's Book of Numbers* (a guide to the sacred numerological traditions of the world) was followed by *In Search of Ancient North Africa* and the text for Don McCullin's photographic study of Roman North Africa and the Levant, *Southern Frontiers*. Barnaby also co-edited a collection of the contemporary travel writing *Ox-Tales* for the charity Oxfam, edited a collection of the travel literature of Marrakech, co-edited a collection of contemporary travel encounters with Islam; *Meetings with Remarkable Muslims*, a collection of English Orientalist verse, *Desert Air*, and a collection of the poetry of place of *London*.

He has almost finished, *A House Divided* a book which looks at conflict zones within the Middle East complicated by the Shia-Sunni schism within Islam. It was meant to be a light introduction but instead grew into a sprawling first draft of over a quarter of a million words. In order to cut such a book back to size, it is vital to turn your attention to something completely different, which led to *A Book Full of Rogersons*.